Day by Day

through the PSALMS

Day by Day

through the PSALMS

C. William Nichols

CHALICE®
PRESS

ST. LOUIS, MISSOURI

Bible quotations, unless otherwise noted, are from the *New Revised Standard Version Bible*, copyright 1989, Division of Christian Education of the National Council of Churches of Christ in the United States of America. Used by permission.

Those quotations marked RSV are from the *Revised Standard Version of the Bible*, copyright 1952, [2nd edition, 1971] by the Division of Christian Education of the National Council of the Churches of Christ in the United States of America. Used by permission. All rights reserved.

Cover photo: © Digital Stock
Cover and interior design: Elizabeth Wright
Art direction: Elizabeth Wright

This book is printed on acid-free, recycled paper.

Visit Chalice Press on the World Wide Web at
www.chalicepress.com

10 9 8 7 6 5 4 3 2 1   03 04 05 06 07 08

Library of Congress Cataloging-in-Publication Data

Nichols, C. William.
  Day by day through the Psalms / by C. William Nichols.
     p. cm.
  ISBN 0-8272-0632-1
  1. Bible. O.T. Psalms—Meditations. I. Title.
  BS1430.54 N53 2003
  242'.5—dc21
                                        2002152172

Printed in the United States of America

This book is lovingly dedicated to
Christian and Bella,
the fresh new growth
of a loving family.

INTRODUCTION

A bit of doggerel, well remembered from childhood, said:

King David and King Solomon
Led merry, merry lives,
With many, many concubines
And many, many wives.
But when old age o'ertook them,
With many, many qualms,
King Solomon wrote the Proverbs, and
Kind David wrote the Psalms.

There is a bit of truth in those lines. While David did not write all the psalms, almost half of them—73 of the 150 psalms—are attributed to the shepherd king. That may mean that he wrote them himself, or that they were written by someone else and attributed to David. And it is possible that more than the 73 clearly identified with David may have come from his mind or from his influence.

But the qualms—certainly David had many, many of them: misgivings, doubts, attacks of conscience, and fears. In fact, the psalms express many of the human faults and frailties to which we are all heir.

The book of Psalms has been called "The People's Bible" because it exposes so many of the experiences and feelings that are woven into the fabric of everyone's lives. Life in its most honest aspects may be found within the pages of the psalms. It's there, warts and all: heights of joy and depths of despair, magnanimous and compassionate concern for others and the most venomous and vitriolic curses to be found anywhere in the Bible. Both temptation and trust, gratitude and antipathy, share the stage in the outpouring of passion expressed in these literary masterpieces.

William Wordsworth once defined poetry as "emotion recollected in tranquility." Such a definition also describes the psalms.

But frequently a psalm that begins with a complaint works its way through the honest assessment of experience to end with a triumphant word of trust. A splendid example of this is the twenty-second psalm, which Jesus knew well enough to quote from the cross. It begins with the mournful cry, "My God, my God, why hast thou forsaken me?" (22:1, RSV), but ends with the assurance, "For he has not despised or abhorred the affliction of the afflicted; and he has not hid his face from him, but has heard, when he cried to him" (22:24, RSV). And although Jesus' agony in the appalling moment on the cross would not permit him to recite the psalm to its triumphant ending, one must believe that his mind and heart reached that comforting conclusion, and it was in that trust that he died.

Surely everyone's list of favorite scriptures would include one or more psalms. Probably the best-loved scripture is the twenty-third psalm, with its familiar images of green pastures, still waters, and the table prepared for us. But every psalm is a gem that provides some inspiration or challenge to everyone who reads it.

My two previous books in this series—*Day by Day through the New Testament: The Gospels* and *Day by Day through the New Testament: Acts to Revelation*—have evoked a most heartening response from readers, for which I am most grateful. That response has reinforced my conviction that people are hungry for Bible study and eager to find a systematic plan for reading the scriptures. This volume on the Psalms also seeks to satisfy the longing that people have expressed to me to find a way to delve into the beautiful poetry of the book of Psalms, and to mine from its riches some of the daily inspiration that the book has provided for centuries to those who undertake a serious study of it.

To add a personal note: Over the nine months of labor that produced this book, I have enjoyed a complete, systematic, and thorough reading of the book of Psalms, from the first word of the first chapter through the last word of the final psalm. It has been a most remarkable experience, and one for which I am grateful. It is my prayer that this little book will aid you in discovering such a blessing in your own life.

God love you, every one,
C. William Nichols

DAY 1
Read Psalm 1

Whether by design or caprice, the grand theme of the entire book of Psalms is conveyed in the first word of Psalm 1. In the original Hebrew it is *asre*. Through the ages biblical translators have searched—without great success—for an accurate English equivalent of that word. The *King James Version* renders it "blessed." More recent scholars have opted for the more colloquial "happy." Although the euphoric state may seem the same however it is achieved, there is an enormous difference in the origin of that blissful experience. "Blessed" clearly implies that the gift of bliss was given by one who had the power to make such a gift, whereas "happy" concludes that the personal joy experienced by a good person depends on the "happen-ness" of the circumstance in which the person is found. In other words, does this personal bliss or joy come from some benevolent source beyond ourselves, or does it result from the roulette of human experiences—good and bad—that fall on us?

What most translators fail to express, however, is the fact that the word is clearly an interjection—an exclamation of astonishment: "What an amazingly happy person!" or "Look how that person has been blessed!"

The implication is clear that when we live in companionship with God, and live the kind of life that honors that association, the result in our lives should be amazingly radiant. No petulant footnotes claiming exemption will be found in our songs of praise to God, no self-pitying whining for easier lives or richer resources.

The apostle Paul had found that life of transcendental happiness, and he poured out his words of joy in his letter to the Philippians: "I know what it is to have little, and I know what it is to have plenty. In any and all circumstances I have learned the secret of being well-fed and of going hungry, of having plenty and of being in need. I can do all things through him who strengthens me" (Philippians 4:12–13). "What an amazingly happy person!" (How blessed! How happy!)

And what was Paul's magnificent secret? It was not his reliance on the "happenstance" of favorable contingencies, but on the unfailing strength and purpose provided by the creator and sustainer of life. Whoever has chosen to live in concord with God's spirit and purpose is like a tree growing beside a stream of fresh water. Neither heat nor drought—nor calamity nor disappointment—can steal the life of the tree or the person whose roots provide constant connection with the source of life.

DAY 2
Read Psalm 2

One is strongly tempted to take one sentence from this psalm, rip it out of its context, frame it in some ornate setting, and hang it on a prominent wall where everyone could see it frequently. Here it is: "He who sits in the heavens laughs" (v. 4). What a magnificent insight into the climate of heaven and the personality of its chief resident!

And it is surely a legitimate understanding of God and God's eternal domain. Who would have a greater right to experience the glad expression of bubbling-over laughter than those who have been given the assurance that never again will there be pain or trouble or guilt or want or fear or death anymore?

In one of Eugene O'Neill's lesser-known plays, *Lazarus Laughed,* the biblical story of the raising of Lazarus is carried into another chapter to show how Lazarus lived during his second span of life. To the disappointment of all who plied him with questions about the heaven that he had visited, he had no words to say—words were futile to report what he had seen. But to every question, Lazarus replied with laughter—not derisive or mocking laughter, but the great, rolling, deep-throated and heart-filled laughter that expressed—more than any words could do—the lunacy of trying to see heavenly things with human eyes.

Rather than trivializing the climate of heaven, the concept of laughter in heaven says something profound and lovely that the blessed children of God have a right to claim.

Unfortunately, this single reference to a laughing God refers to the derision or ridicule with which the great God must surely regard the tiny trophies of our effort and the petty preoccupations of our pretensions. The psalmist depicts the highest councils of human politics and the futility of trying to find community and peace through rebellions and various rearrangements of the temporary holders of political power. All are like children playing real estate, "buying and selling" property that belongs to their parents. Whatever their pretenses, the land belongs to their father and mother, and at the end of the day, that ownership will be made clear. But during the long day, the patient tolerance of their parents limits their response to an indulgent chuckle.

So God chuckles at the futile machinations of our human efforts to achieve our utopias. But it is well for us to remember that this is, after all, God's world, and God is ultimately in control here. And it is a tiny measure of our glorious hope that God's response to our frailties is more an indulgent chuckle than a thunderbolt of condemnation.

DAY 3
Read Psalm 3

During the Second World War the people of London were subjected to devastating air raids. There seemed to be no escape from them, and no shelter provided absolute security. Few people could sleep well at night with such frightening possibilities. But one old woman never sought the refuge of a shelter and always seemed to sleep peacefully, even when the bombs were falling. Asked how she could sleep so soundly under such circumstances, she replied, "I read in the psalms that 'he that keepeth thee will not slumber' (Psalm 121:3, KJV), and I figure, what's the use of the both of us staying awake?"

Such was the tranquil confidence of the writer of this psalm. David is given the "byline" here, but the introductory attribution could also mean that this was a psalm written in remembrance of David's trust in God, or that it was the sort of prayer David might have prayed.

Certainly the great shepherd king of Israel had both the ability to create beautiful psalms and the frequent experience of finding himself in situations in which his inner turmoil and fear begged for release. His enemies were many and vicious; his own family turned against him, with his own beloved son Absalom leading the rebellion. Even his dependable faith in God, which had provided comfort and confidence in many difficult situations, was under attack from those who did not share his faith.

This psalm has a most provocative outline. The first half focuses on the dangers and trials that face the psalmist. The second half concentrates on the dependable goodness of God and the ultimate triumph of those who trust in God. What joins the two halves together and accounts for the dramatic change in tone? It is the simple sentence, "I lie down and sleep; I wake again, for the LORD sustains me" (3:5). Many Christian people have had that same experience. We go to bed hounded by anxieties and fears, needing sleep but unable to find that blessed relief that "knits up the raveled sleeve of care."

But if in our faith in God's dependable goodness we can turn it all over to the Creator, we find that healing balm of restful sleep that restores our strength and renews our confidence.

Keep your Bible on your nightstand, and the next time anxieties deprive you of sleep, reach for your Bible and read Psalm 3. You may find—as David surely did—that "[God] gives sleep to his beloved" (Psalm 127:2).

Even for the most deeply committed, faith is still a candle in the wind, its flickering light suggesting that no one can be assured of it as a permanent possession locked up tight in a treasure box. In fact, protecting a lit candle from the wind would deprive it of its very breath. A strong faith is not one that has not been tested, but one that has gone through periods of despair and doubt but remains–in some tiny degree–in control of your will. And faith does not require a placid garden in which to grow, or a calm sea on which to be launched. Faith may sing the "Hallelujah" chorus at times, but it may also lament, "Nobody knows the troubles I've seen!" Both Job in the Old Testament and John the Baptist in the New remind us that valorous faith frequently finds birth through the labor pains of real suffering and sorrow.

But life's vicissitudes do not give us an automatic pass to sainthood. While some may come through their troubles *better* people, others facing the same array of adversities come through it all as *bitter* people.

Above all, don't let either your sufferings or your doubts deprive you of the most valuable resource with which to deal with those foes. Although some of the Psalms shock us by the indignant accusations hurled by the psalmists against a seemingly absent or unhearing God, surely God would rather we voice our complaints than allow our sulking to corrode our relationship with the Creator.

Indeed, one of the most frequent paradigms by which the psalms are patterned is to begin with a bitter cry of disappointment in God, then work through that experience to find, in the end, the ultimate triumph of faith and the resolution of the problem.

This means, then, that faith must always be a process, not a possession; a pilgrimage, not a parade.

Even when it seems that heaven is vacant and no one hears our prayers, God is in the process of answering. Even when the darkness is so palpable it seems positively permanent, God is creating the sunrise that will ultimately conquer it.

So the psalmist advises us, "when you are disturbed, do not sin" (v. 4). Continue to do what you know is right and good for you to do–even though it may seem futile–because through such honoring of your faith, even in the worst of times, you are giving God the materials with which to create the salvation you seek.

DAY 5
Read Psalm 5

After two psalms clearly identified as evening prayers, here is a morning prayer. It is not, however, a "beginning of the day" setting of sights and enlisting of divine help for the way ahead, but a midday "pause for refreshment" and a reminder, in the thick of demands and problems, of the intent with which the day began.

How can this be true? We must bear in mind that in the Hebrew mind, the twenty-four-hour day begins at sunset. The Sabbath day begins with an evening meal. When the writer of Genesis reported the calendar of events of the creation, he did not summarize each day's achievements by writing, "and there was morning and there was evening, one day," but rather, "there was evening and there was morning, the first day" (Genesis 1:5). Or "And there was evening and there was morning, the second day" (Genesis 1:8). And so the pattern continues through each of the six days of God's creative accomplishment—evening first, then morning.

Morning, then, was a time for midpoint assessment and evaluation, and it presented an opportunity to compare actual accomplishment with original intent.

A simple question may be useful to ask oneself in the thick of life's struggles and efforts: "If I get where I'm going, where will I be?" If you follow the same road your feet are now pressing, will you wind up, at day's end, where you really wanted to go? If you continue to develop the same qualities of character your present attitudes and actions are leading you toward, will you have become, at life's end, the person you wanted to be?

It's a good question to ask at midday (or midlife, or in the middle of a career): "If I get where I'm going, where will I be?"

The psalmist, in evaluating where he was in the fulfillment of his life's intentions, concluded that only in faithfulness to God could he find the clarity of vision and strength for achievement that he wanted. Despite occasional appearances to the contrary, everything that works against the holy will of God is living on borrowed time; evildoers will get their comeuppance ultimately; the wrong will fail and the right prevail. God will not forever tolerate the reign of godlessness. Live by those principles, and you will get results; try to live in rebellion against them, and you will get consequences.

And that's something worth reminding ourselves of, in the heat and busyness of the day.

DAY 6
Read Psalm 6

The portrait the Bible paints of David is a striking study in paradoxes. He was rugged enough, as a youth, to defend his flock of sheep against wild animals; confident enough, as a young man, to stride onto a field of battle with only a slingshot in his arsenal to face an armed and armored giant; and masterful enough to rule a contentious nation so proficiently that even centuries later he occupies the most honored niche in that nation's hall of heroes. That was the public David.

But look, now, at that same David when the palace doors are closed for the night, the adoring populace has departed, and the king removes his royal crown and goes to bed.

Can this be the same man, now weeping like a frightened little boy, terrified at the thought of enemies at the gates, intimidated by his own inadequacies, and almost afraid to approach God in prayer? For he knows–though no one else may–how little he really deserves the adulation of his followers. And he has the terrible suspicion that his enemies may know him better than his friends do. And worst of all, he knows, all too well, how little he deserves the blessings for which he begs God.

Although it shocks us to face it, most of us would have to concede that there is a bit of the same contradiction in us. We would not want to call it hypocrisy, for our intention is not to deceive. But there is a bit of pride in every one of us that wants to "put our best foot forward" and not "hang our dirty linen out in public." But when we are alone–perhaps when we lie down at night–the silence accuses us, and the darkness threatens us.

But perhaps what made David a man after God's own heart was the fact that this walking contradiction of a man found, when he entered that torture chamber that his solitude had become, that God went with him into the torture chamber. And–glory of all glories– this perfect God, whose holiness is seamless and beyond compare, is willing to accept our prayers, even though they come from hands and hearts that are still smudged with the muck of our failures and weaknesses. "The LORD has heard my supplication," David said, "the LORD accepts my prayer" (v. 9).

When Jesus taught us to "go into your room and shut the door and pray to your Father who is in secret" (Matthew 6:6), perhaps he was urging us to experience, as David did, the joy of letting God into the darkest and most frightening places of our lives. For it is in those places in our lives where we need God the most.

DAY 7
Read Psalm 7

A recent Associated Press article related the sad story of a woman who was tripped by a wire in her backyard, and in the ensuing fall her leg was broken. That alone is a bit tragic, but even more unfortunate is the subplot of this little drama. The woman was an avid gardener and especially prized the tomatoes in her backyard garden. But neighborhood children teased her by picking the tomatoes before they were ripe and leaving them on the ground. To guard against this juvenile mischief, she strung an electric wire around her little garden to give a shocking warning to anyone who came near. And it was her own threatening invention that caused her downfall.

Such is the mournful irony depicted in the verse that says the wicked "make a pit, digging it out, and fall into the hole that they have made" (v. 15). There is a play on words in the original Hebrew here, which says literally, "he digs a pit and the pit pits him." And that expresses a fact of life in this world that we cannot escape. We cannot do evil without some of the evil we do staying with us. You cannot sling mud at another without becoming muddy in the process.

There is an axiomatic phrase—rarely heard these days—that refers to being "hoisted by one's own petard." Many people use the phrase without really understanding the act to which it refers. The reference is to an explosive device used in England many years ago that was useful in breaking down walls or locked doors. The problem with the petard, however, was that it had such a short igniting device that often the one lighting it was blown up by his own destructive actions. Hence, "hoist by one's own petard" means to be damaged by one's own effort to damage someone else.

Be warned by this reminder in the psalm that you cannot hate without becoming a hater. You cannot do violence to another without becoming a violent person. And to provide a happy corollary, you cannot do good to another without becoming, in the process, a more blessed person yourself. A greeting card verse attributed to Helen Steiner Rice expresses this thought: "You can't give a rose, all fragrant with dew, without some of the fragrance remaining with you."

The self-defeating action described in this psalm has been the basis of many slapstick comedy sequences. And it may be funny when it happens to someone else, but when it happens to us, it is sometimes a costly lesson. Our own actions either bless or betray us.

DAY 8
Read Psalm 8

There is no more lofty literature in the Bible than this psalm, which poetically links together two of the most profound human mysteries: What is God? and What are we?

At first the contrast between the majestic God and the frail creatures of the Earth seems an unbridgeable gulf. Ponder the astonishing dimensions of the universe! Who can measure the circumference of the universe, or weigh the mass of it, or conceive the mysterious network of gravity that holds together the whole intricate arrangement? Such astral complexities reduce us to children, asking innocently, "Twinkle, twinkle little star, how I wonder what you are!"

An old word that was reborn to colloquial use makes the statement in a song from several years ago: "Our God Is an Awesome God." Sun, moon, and stars; planets, galaxies, and universes beyond the reach of eye or mind proclaim that the God who created it all is powerful, surpassing our imagination.

Now think of that awesome God, who is not too busy running the universe to neglect the tiniest seedling in the garden that is praying hard to be a flower. And every human being—frail as we are, prone to rebellion as we are—is the object of this God's passionate concern. What a paradox! The hymn writer of "Beneath the Cross of Jesus" pondered this contrast:

> And from my stricken heart with tears two wonders I confess:
> the wonders of redeeming love and my unworthiness.

And what is it that makes us worthy of God's concern? It is the totally unearned and undeserved gift of partnership with this awesome God. God creates the Earth, then in an act of incredible trust, leaves us in charge of it. God gives us *dominion*. That word means the right to rule. A part of God's own nature is born in us: the right to decide, the freedom of will. And God leaves this divine gift intact, despite our petty experimentations with rebellion and betrayal. No matter what we do, we are held secure in the grip of a great love that will not let us go.

So the psalm celebrates the God of the human family, and the human family of this God. And there is an unmistakable grandeur in both. God has made you a child of the divine. Claim your inheritance!

The ancient Hebrews attached great importance to names. The name was thought to be the essence of the person or object thereby identified. And to know the name of something or someone implied that a relationship existed between the "knower" and the "knowee." When God instructed Adam to name the animals in the creation narratives, the implication was that Adam (and his descendants) would have dominion over the animals thus named. When Jacob wrestled with that mysterious adversary all night at the ford of the Jabbok, the one thing each opponent demanded of the other was "What is your name?" To obey that demand would have been the equivalent of "saying uncle." To give your name to your adversary would be putting yourself under the enemy's power. The real essence of that story is that there was a time–long delayed–in which Jacob finally came to terms with his God. He had been the aggressor and had tried to manipulate God, as he had successfully manipulated everyone else. But at last the strong-willed Jacob found one he could not bully or exploit. And in that historic showdown, Jacob surrendered his name (and his will) to God, but God steadfastly declined to reveal God's name to Jacob.

So Jacob came out of that experience a chastened and transformed man, a permanent limp reminding him that he had met his match in God.

One's name represents one's essence, one's identity.

For that reason, many reverent Jews have been reluctant to speak the name of God aloud, or even to write it out in full. In many Hebrew writings the name of God is abbreviated by a single letter, to ensure that the name of God is not blasphemed.

One who reveres the name of the Lord cannot help but be shocked by the frequency and the casualness with which the Lord's name is taken in vain in modern movies, television programs, and other public media, thus reducing a name of exquisite beauty and majestic power to a flippant bit of profanity. And the punishment for such a misuse of the holy name is that those who misuse it are robbing themselves of a source of great power and inspiration for their lives.

For those who know the name of God, and speak it often with the reverence and understanding that it deserves, have declared by their action that they put their trust in the one named. And as the psalm declares, such people will not be forsaken by God, for the Lord knows them and, in an act of holy grace, gives them the Holy Spirit as a sign of divine favor.

DAY 10

The mother of eleven children was frequently asked—sometimes in jest, other times seriously—which of her children she loved the most. The questioner always expected her to reply, "I love them all the same." But she would frequently shock her hearers by saying, "I love most the one who's sick, until he's well, and the one who's gone, until he's back home." While the scriptures make it quite clear that God is not prejudiced in favor of any persons or groups of persons ("the wisdom from above is...without a trace of partiality" [James 3:17]), it is also clear that God has a very special concern for the poor, the oppressed, the unjustly-dealt-with, and those who suffer innocently. And while there is a certain justice to be discerned in the suffering of the wicked, it is difficult to understand why bad things happen to good people.

This psalm has much to say about the injustices suffered by the orphans and the widows, the oppressed and the poor. And in each case, the need for justice for those people is seen as a divine cause. "Where is God?" the atheists gloat. And even the friends of God lament, "Why, O LORD, do you stand far off? Why do you hide yourself in times of trouble?" (v. 1).

An Indian mystic tells of standing on a street of Calcutta one day, appalled by the ocean of misery all around him: the sick, the dying, the poor, the disabled, the suffering. He cried out his indignation, "Lord, why don't you do something about all this?" And he recalls that he heard a voice answering his accusation, "I most certainly have done something about it: I made you."

Sometimes people cite the undeserved miseries of the unfortunate as justification for their disbelief in God. "How can I believe in a God who would allow such terrible things to happen to innocent people?" they reason. Rather, they should see such instances of sorrow and suffering as proof that we have failed to complete God's plan for a world of Shalom, where justice is fulfilled for everyone, and every need is met. Eden is what God intended for us; the world of crime, war, disease, poverty, and injustice is what we have made of it.

But until God's perfect kingdom comes, in which there will be justice for all, there are evidences, here and there, of how the Spirit of God, operating in hearts that are tender to human hurt and responsive to God's intent, can make a genuine difference in the world around us. At the very least, by our own divinely commissioned efforts, we can be a part of the solution and not a part of the problem.

DAY 11
Read Psalm 11

When one's religious faith is under siege, there are two possible courses of action: to *resign* or to *re-sign.*

The problem described in the eleventh Psalm is one that has been a familiar experience for religious leaders throughout history: At the very moment when faith needs to be the strongest come the most insidious temptations to abandon faith altogether. Think of John the Baptist, facing execution in Herod's dungeon, having only one comfort and hope to equip him for his ordeal: his faith in God's Messiah. But it was at that very moment when he needed his faith the most that he felt his certainty evaporating. But instead of resigning his faith at that critical time, he went back to school, enrolling in Discipleship 101, studying the works of Jesus. He sent messengers to Jesus to ask of him, "'Are you the one who is to come, or are we to wait for another?' Jesus answered them, 'Go and tell John what you hear and see: the blind receive their sight, the lame walk, the lepers are cleansed, the deaf hear, the dead are raised, and the poor have good news brought to them'" (Matthew 11:3–5). And although the gospel writer fails to complete the story of John's ordeal, one can easily conclude that from this refresher course in the Christian faith, John drew the strength and assurance he needed to go to his death as a victor, and not as a victim. Instead of resigning his commission as a disciple, he signed up again!

So in the clutches of whatever pain or problem or anguish gripped the soul of the psalmist, he was advised by his own "miserable comforters" to "flee like a bird to the mountains" (v. 1). And since Jerusalem was nestled in a mountainscape, running away in any direction would take one to the mountains. So the perfidious advice to the troubled psalmist was "get out of town. Leave your troubles behind! Your faith is too great a burden to you. Lay it down and run away! Resign! With a friend like your God, who needs enemies?"

But instead the psalmist re-signed his commission as a believer. And he began by reminding himself of the catechism of his faith: Our God is a righteous God, who will always stand by those who attempt to reflect God's righteousness in their own actions.

Momentary appearances to the contrary, God's people are on the winning team.

DAY 12
Read Psalm 12

One of the most painful aspects of spiritual discouragement is that it narrows the focus of our attention until we can see nothing and no one beyond ourselves. We begin to feel that the whole world is against us and that there is no one left to help us. "There is no longer anyone who is godly," the psalmist moaned, "the faithful have disappeared from humankind" (v. 1).

Such a complaint recalls for us the despair of the prophet Elijah, who once endured such a time. In self-pity and despondency he lay down under a broom tree in the wilderness of Beersheba, wishing he could die, and then spent the night in a cave. He hurled his complaint against the heavens, "I, even I only, am left!" (1 Kings 19:10, RSV). But God patiently led him to recovery through a simple set of instructions. God told Elijah:

Look up! Elijah was so concerned about what he saw around him that he had forgotten what was above him. When the outlook is bleak, someone has suggested, try the uplook!

Get up! Inactivity breeds despair. No matter how bewildered or discouraged you might be, there is always at least one thing you know would be right and good for you to do. And until you have done that, you have no right to complain that "there is nothing more I can do."

Fill up! If your tank of spiritual resources is empty, you obviously need to go to a spiritual filling station. Read your Bible. Pray. Worship at God's house. God sent Elijah to Mount Horeb (Sinai), where his religion was founded. God sent him back to the basics of his faith, to have his faith lifted. It's a spiritual homecoming that we all need from time to time.

Link up! Elijah thought he was the only righteous person left in the world, that he was alone in the battle he was called on to wage. But God widened Elijah's view to see that there were at least seven thousand others in Israel who shared his faith, even in that time of widespread apostasy. Elijah needed the strength and courage that would result from his joining forces with people of like mind and faith.

So the psalmist found the recovery of his faith in taking the initiative to do the things that would restore his faith and confidence. And the very next sentence of Elijah's biography tells of how God sent him a helper–Elisha–who helped him bear his burden.

God has many glorious surprises waiting for you, but none of them are found on the ground under the broom tree.

DAY 13
Read Psalm 13

Some of the world's most beautiful music has been produced in times of distress and sorrow. Think of the spirituals, which gave expression to those trapped in the seemingly hopeless prison of slavery. Consider the blues songs of the next generations, in which those who finally discovered release from slavery found themselves in a world that had many more injustices and cruelties to be suffered.

Centuries earlier, in a lonely prison cell in the hostile city of Philippi, Paul and Silas celebrated their unjust incarceration by lifting up their voices in song. "About midnight," the scripture says (Acts 16:25), at the darkest hour, these indefatigable stalwarts of the faith lifted up their voices in song. It didn't matter much whether their song was "Nobody Knows the Trouble I've Seen," or the "Hallelujah" chorus, it must have been music to God's ears, and it must have made a powerful statement to the Philippian jailer, who shortly thereafter became an adherent of the faith that prompted songs at midnight.

So, as must be said of many of the psalms, this mournful dirge was squeezed out by some painfully cruel exigencies. "How long?" Four times the question is accusingly hurled at God. But it is worth noting that though the psalmist has complaints against God, the conversation with God continues! And whether it is a sigh or a song, any communication with God strengthens the connection and the relationship.

But such agonizing questions deserve answers! Suppose you were called on to rewrite this psalm and to compose, between the lines of this lament, God's replies. Is it puerile to believe that God did, indeed, answer those questions? How would God respond to the accusing demands: "How long will you forget me? How long will you hide your face from me?"

Isn't it possible that God answered those—and a million other—agonizing questions of the human family, in the miracle of grace we call the Incarnation? Jesus was God's message to a frequently bewildered and discouraged world: "I know you; I care about you; I will never leave you nor forsake you. And I know what you need, and I give it to you freely."

Someone has imagined a seeker asking God, "How much do you love me?" In reply God stretched out his arms and said, "This much," and died.

DAY 14
Read Psalm 14

In the black-and-white theology of the psalmist, God was the source of all good, and all evil represented the absence of God. An evil believer or a good atheist was an oxymoron too contradictory to be believed. Unfortunately in the real world we live in, there are confusing shades of gray that mask the truth, and the human experience doesn't always clearly demonstrate the eternal verities—at least, not in the short term. Truth often requires a grander podium than our attention span to declare its authenticity.

But in its ultimate consideration, the axiom set forth in this psalm is a dependable basis for a successful life in this world. Where there is God, there is good; and where God is absent, so is good.

To be sure, there are enough apparent exceptions to this rule to give the atheists and agnostics fodder for their sophistries. Think of the news reports of the Eagle Scout who massacres fellow students at school or the Sunday school teacher or church deacon or treasurer who absconds with church funds and runs away with the organist. But thank God such incidents are still rare enough to be newsworthy. For every good person who goes bad, there are dozens of good people who manage—year in and year out—to uphold the standards of decency, often in the face of great temptation or depleted spiritual resources. But while every struggle with temptation is still enough of a horse race to make the outcome less than certain, most of us have become so accustomed to regular victories that we forget that we have been involved in a contest.

Despite those nagging questions that rebound in our minds the way spicy foods return to our digestive system, this is, at the core of its being, a world created by God, loved by God, visited by God, and saved by God. And God has put far too much into this world to let it go without a heroic struggle the likes of which we have never seen. "He's Got the Whole World in His Hands," as the song says, and while we may occasionally flirt with other identities, we know—deep down inside—that we belong to God, and God will not let us go.

But while such truths are demonstrable over the course of centuries, a moment may be too small a vessel to yield such a distillate. As Reinhold Niebuhr once said, "I'll be a pessimist with you day by day, if you'll be an optimist with me, eon by eon."

DAY 15

Read Psalm 15

A new resident of an apartment building in New York City realized that she would be expected, at Christmas time, to proffer a monetary gift to the building's doorman, elevator operator, and various other service people who attended to the needs of the residents. But this new occupant was not aware of the usual amount of such gratuities. Not wanting to be out of step with her neighbors, the she asked the doorman, "What is the average gift the residents give you at Christmas time?" The doorman promptly answered, "The average gift would be one hundred dollars." The resident was surprised, but complied in the gift she subsequently gave. The day after Christmas the doorman was full of gratitude. "In my twenty-five years of service as a doorman here," he said, "you are the first person who has ever come up to the average."

David's list of qualifications for those who would enter God's house also seems to set too high a standard to be universally applied. Imagine what would result if church attendees showed up at church some Sunday and were met at the door by an examining committee that would check off their compliance with the qualifications set forth in this psalm. If this is intended as a portrait of the average worshiper, surely few could claim to come up to the average!

Of course, God's house is worthy of such reverence. Our modern disregard for the traditional holiness of certain things or places notwithstanding, one must surely realize that in a world in which there is nothing sacred, there is also little piety. But it is also true that we rob ourselves of great spiritual power when we glorify something beyond our ability to grasp and use it.

The church, then, as a building or as an institution or as a community of believers, must never get beyond the reach of even the least qualified who might seek to enter. The church was never intended to be a museum for saints, but a clinic for sinners. And if one must achieve a certain moral uprightness or spiritual depth before entering the presence of God, who, then, would be found worthy of that holy presence?

It is an attribute of the grace of divine favor that although God deserves us to be at our best, God is perfectly willing to accept us at our worst. And those human doorkeepers who see their primary function as keeping out of the kingdom those they deem not worthy of such inclusion, may one day discover that one of the chief characteristics of those abiding in the divine presence is being God's open heart and open door to those who are the least qualified to enter.

DAY 16
Read Psalm 16

___

It would be easy to pass over this psalm with scant attention to its importance. It would also be most unfortunate. It should be noted that this psalm is twice quoted by early Christian leaders. Peter cited this psalm in his sermon on Pentecost, using its beautiful wording to express the Christian's joy and confidence as a result of Christ's resurrection (Acts 2:25–28). And Paul used this psalm in his great sermon at Antioch to signify the hope by which a Christian lives (Acts 13:35). It is clear, then, that this psalm was a favorite scripture for Jewish and early Christian believers.

It is also a psalm with which many of us can identify, for it reports (without boasting, only acknowledging with gratitude) that God has blessed us with great material gifts: "The LORD is my chosen portion and my cup" (v. 5). (Recall the symbolism used in the twenty-third Psalm's "my cup overflows.") "The boundary lines have fallen for me in pleasant places" (v. 6). As modern-day American Christians, we must acknowledge, with some humility and wonder, that by accident of birth we have been given a rich inheritance. The boundary lines of our land run through the richest real estate in the world. "I have a goodly heritage," David says (v. 6). And which one of us can claim that we have not?

But a small phrase in this psalm discloses one of the believer's chief sources of inspiration and spiritual instruction. "In the night also my heart instructs me" (v. 7). Here is a secret that many Christians through the ages have learned and practiced in their spiritual lives. During the day they study or meditate or think about the scriptures, little realizing that in doing so they are laying up a rich store of spiritual strength and inspiration. And it is at night, when we turn off our active thought processes, that those spiritual truths rise to our consciousness, so that even when we are unaware of the process, the teachings of the holy scriptures continue to strengthen and prepare us for the day ahead.

Many people have adopted, as their prayer exercise before falling asleep at night, a pattern by which they visualize opening the lid at the top of their heads and examining everything that has entered that place of awareness during the day. Many thoughts, memories, and resentments may have been deposited there. The unworthy things should be removed by consigning them to God for disposal. But also in our minds is the awareness of blessings, gifts, and favors that God has given us along the way, and fresh realizations of truth. Those things should be put back into our minds with gratitude, and left there to grow and to speak up, in our sleep, to instruct us.

DAY 17
Read Psalm 17

It does seem a bit presumptuous, doesn't it? By what right does the psalmist implore the great God of all the heavens and the earth to "guard me as the apple of [your] eye" (v. 8)? Maybe God has other plans, with other people at the center of divine attention. Does "*the* apple" mean that David wanted to be the one and only favorite son and heir of the Holy One, or would David have conceded the possibility that God might love him and others, too, with the same extravagant love? Maybe God has a whole bushel basket full of "apples of the eye" or a whole orchard of such favored offspring. Perhaps "God's favorite" is a distinction that awaits everyone who accepts and lives by it.

And maybe being a focal point of God's attention is not so much a privilege as an obligation. Tevye, the poverty-stricken milkman in the musical *Fiddler on the Roof,* laments, "Being poor may not be a disgrace, but it's no great honor, either." And recounting all the instances of persecution against the Jewish people, Tevye concedes that they are God's chosen people, but wonders, "Why doesn't God choose someone else once in awhile?"

The Hebrew word translated "apple" is literally "the little person," and usually referred to the pupil of the eye. If you stand close to someone and look into the eye, you will see "a little person" (yourself) reflected in the pupil. So the apple of God's eye is the person you see when you come close to God and see yourself in God's attention.

How it changes our attitudes toward the difficulties we face when we know that God keeps us in sight at all times! Think what it would do to your fears of the future if you knew that God was watching you, keeping you at the center of attention. That's what being "the apple of God's eye" really means.

A little girl learned her memory verse at Sunday school, which said, "Thou God seest me" (Genesis 16:13, KJV). But instead of comforting her, the verse frightened her. Did those words mean that God was constantly watching her to catch her in some kind of mischief? Finally, her parents retranslated that verse to give their daughter a real understanding of its meaning. Thereafter she found comfort in the new version: "God loves you so much God can't keep his eyes off you!"

And when you come close to God, you will see that the great Lord of all creation has you in the loving focus of attention.

A small boy had gone up on the roof to retrieve his kite, which had become entangled in a television antenna. But he lost his footing and began to roll down the pitched roof, toward the edge. In terror, he cried out his prayer, "Lord, save me!" And just then, a nail protruding from the edge of the roof caught his shirt and held him safe. "Never mind, Lord," he said, "I got hung up on a nail."

As fervent as our petitions for help might be, we are prone to leave God out of our consideration when our prayers are answered. How many are our pleas for help; how few are our prayers of gratitude!

Psalm 18 is specifically identified as David's expression of gratitude to God for bringing him safely through a day of great danger from his enemies, and specifically from the murderous rage of King Saul. The purist might complain that David's exultation in his special powers to overcome his enemies smacks of self-aggrandizement. And some of his words do seem a bit boastful: "I can crush a troop…I can leap over a wall." But he is always careful to credit the Giver for such gifts: "*By you* I can crush a troop, and *by my God* I can leap over a wall" (v. 29).

And if David was given to exulting in his victories, he was equally candid in reporting his disgrace and dishonor when he failed. Few writings anywhere can approach the depth of regret and contrition expressed in Psalm 51, in which David freely confessed his sin and acknowledged the extent of his guilt.

Like an ardent suitor who exhausts the language dreaming up terms of affection to call his sweetheart, David runs through the lexicon of holy names by which to praise God: my strength, my rock, my fortress, my deliverer, my God, my shield, the horn of my salvation, my stronghold. Like the hymn writer wishing for "a thousand tongues to sing my great Redeemer's praise," David exhausts the language and still finds the goodness of God beyond the reach of human definition.

But each of these references to God is modified by the personal possessive pronoun *my*. It is a marvelous thought that God is strength, rock, fortress, deliverer. But more wonderful still is the realization that such a God is *my* God, and all the powers and attributes of this many-splendored God are pledged to protect and bless those who are God's own.

DAY 19
Read Psalm 19

Reading Psalm 19 is like reluctantly going to a party, afraid that you will not know anyone present. But immediately on entering you begin to see many old friends and others with whom you have become acquainted on other occasions. Just inside the door you see someone introduced to you by the composer Felix Mendelssohn. How beautifully he introduces this friend, "The Heavens Are Telling" the glory of God! That tune is a part of your repertoire of music, but you didn't realize you would be running into it here in this psalm.

And there's that charming depiction of the sun as a bridegroom, emerging from his tent, adorned and radiant for his bride, or like a strong man daily running a race with vigor and enthusiasm, sprinting effortlessly from the sunrise end of the earth to the sunset point. What a powerful picture, and how unerringly it points to the genius of the Creator!

Then, at this party of discovery, you see the six sisters of the family of divine instruction. You know they are sisters because of their family resemblance. Each follows the pattern set by the first: "The law of the Lord is perfect, reviving the soul" (v. 7). Together they remind us that God speaks to us in wisdom that nourishes the soul.

Finally, there is the prayer sung in unison by all present—and by millions of people in all the years since who have felt the responsibility of communicating God's truth to others:

Let the words of my mouth and the meditation of my heart
be acceptable to you,
O LORD, my rock and my redeemer. (v. 14)

Few passages of the Old Testament are so packed with powerful and indelible images that cling to the memory. Taken as a whole, the psalm is all about the magnificence of God's communication—not only the form it takes but the power it conveys. And for those of us who would seek to follow God's example by communicating the truth through teaching, preaching, or simply advising or witnessing to a friend, we are surely humbled by the vast gulf between our efforts to pass on the truth, and God's. All we can do is pray that both our words and the thought processes that produce those words may please God and achieve their intended purpose.

And if, from time to time, we actually succeed in this, it is because God has been present in that process, to give us strength (our rock) and forgiveness when we fail (our redeemer).

DAY 20
Read Psalm 20

For centuries loyal subjects have cheered their monarchs in such incantations as "God Save the King!" or "Long Live the King!" Even the apostle Paul charged, "I urge that supplications, prayers, intercessions, and thanksgivings be made for everyone, for kings and all who are in high positions" (1 Timothy 2:1–2). It is not that kings, presidents, and other political leaders are more worthy of such divine help than lesser folk, but they carry in their lives the destinies of their peoples.

Such was especially the case in the time of David, who is said to have written this psalm. If the son of Jesse did, indeed, compose this psalm, it was clearly before he had ascended to the throne, while Saul was yet king. Despite his loyalty to his monarch, David suffered much from Saul. And because of Saul's mental and emotional instability and paranoia, he was not a good king. Still, when Saul went forth to lead his troops in battle, David prayed this prayer for him, beseeching the Lord to give Saul help from God's holy sanctuary.

The people of Israel who joined in the singing of this prayer, whether they held Saul in high regard or not, would have had a real stake in the king's victory. If he went down to defeat, all his people might be subjected to servitude, confiscation of their properties, or even death. So whether his personal attributes merited God's blessing or not, the people prayed for him.

But the psalm ends with a ringing assurance that the people's prayers for their king and nation will be answered, and that God will assure them of victory. How could they be so sure? It was because they believed their cause was just, and they put their trust not in chariots or horses, but in their God.

Unfortunately, neither those people nor the more recent people of America have really put their complete confidence in God. While we find some comfort in our unofficial national motto, "In God We Trust," we still want larger armies and more destructive weapons than our neighbors. During the Second World War a popular song expressed our bifurcated commitment: "Praise the Lord and Pass the Ammunition." But if forced to choose between these two sources of power, which do you suppose we would opt for?

Might and right battle for our allegiance even in our own personal lives, as Jesus pointed out in his Sermon on the Mount: "No one can serve two masters; for a slave will either hate the one and love the other, or be devoted to the one and despise the other. You cannot serve God and wealth [mammon]" (Matthew 6:24). Which are you depending on for your victories: horses and chariots or faith and righteousness?

DAY 21
Read Psalm 21

Piecing together the fragmentary records and clues presented to us in several of the books of the Old Testament, we can conclude that David lived to the age of seventy years, reigning for forty of those years as king of Israel. Although this psalm and the one before it seem to have a great deal in common (both 20 and 21 being "royal" psalms, beseeching God's help for the king), the twentieth was surely written when David was a youth, asking God's blessing on Saul. The twenty-first Psalm was almost certainly written by David toward the end of his life, about himself. "He asked you for life," the psalmist writes of his own request to God for longevity, "you gave it to him—length of days forever and ever" (v. 4). One does not thank God for long life at the age of thirty or fifty, but surely at the age of seventy or thereabouts, the thought tugs at the mind: "God has surely blessed me by giving me so many years to live." And it is also at that mature age that one begins to think beyond the horizon of this world to ponder the greater length of life—"forever and ever."

So the aging David reflects on a life crowned with astonishing blessings. God had given him all the desires of his heart. There is a golden crown on his head, and splendor and majesty are symbolized in all the trophies of his achievement.

But such temporal and material blessings pale beside the treasure of God's own presence in his heart. David knows the joy of daily companionship with God. Such, unfortunately, was not always the case. As a hot-blooded young man, he betrayed his covenant with God in his grievous sin of adultery with Bathsheba. And he compounded his guilt by having Bathsheba's husband, Uriah, killed so that no one would discover the shame of his dalliance with Bathsheba. And for this (and perhaps other) sins, David paid the price of his own shame and remorse and his feeling of having created an unbridgeable chasm between himself and God. "Do not cast me away from your presence!" David pled (Psalm 51:11), his guilt convincing him that he did not deserve the joy of God's presence.

But even the most egregious transgressions cannot deny God entrance into the heart that is open and contrite. So now, toward the end of his life, David reviews his past—all the good and the bad and the in-between—and for it all he concludes, "through the steadfast love of the Most High" (v. 7), he shall not be moved!

DAY 22
Read Psalm 22

Jesus frequently drew inspiration and strength by recalling scriptures that he had memorized. He withstood all three temptations in the wilderness by recalling quotations from the book of Deuteronomy, which he had probably learned in his synagogue school or perhaps from his devout parents. Within the wide range of the repertoire of scriptures his study had harvested, there was something that would address any occasion, speak to any problem.

But how could Jesus have guessed, when he learned Psalm 22, that there would come a crisis in which the words of that ancient lament would be painfully appropriate? "My God, my God, why have you forsaken me?" (v. 1). As understandable as that cry of despair might have been when the psalmist faced whatever exigency wrenched those words from his heart, surely Jesus, the faithful and unshakable believer, would never sink to such a depth!

But we shortchange our understanding of the Incarnation when we suppose that there was any human weakness or temptation to which he was not subjected. If that evil extremity that he suffered on the cross did not evoke such thoughts and emotions as the psalmist voiced, then we are guilty either of underestimating the horror he faced on that bitter day, hanging on a cross of pain and defeat, or of robbing Jesus of the humanity that gives us comfort in our own times of distress.

Yes, Jesus did suffer—indescribably—and yes, Jesus did feel desperately alone. And yes, Jesus surely must have felt—in that literally God-forsaken experience—that there was no help available to him.

But there occurred to Jesus this psalm, which he knew from childhood and which described his circumstances in a torturous lament. And Jesus quoted the psalm aloud, to speak to his own soul, and to make his last verbal witness to those who stood around the cross. But his weakened state garbled his words, so that the executioners heard his words "Eli, Eli" and thought he was calling for Elijah. And although his weakness and pain would not permit him to complete his recitation of the psalm, doubtless his mind recalled the resolution later in the psalm: "He did not despise or abhor the affliction of the afflicted; he did not hide his face from me, but heard when I cried to him" (v. 24). And it was in the confidence of that assurance that Jesus died.

DAY 23
Read Psalm 23

Many people can quote–even if it is the only scripture they can quote–this beautiful psalm, which has been called the loveliest poem ever written. Many whole books have been written about this literary and spiritual gem, and it is unlikely that a few words in reflection on this psalm will contribute any new light. But give some thought today to a grammatical peculiarity that might be a key to a new understanding of the whole psalm.

As scholars have long recognized, the first nine lines of the psalm and the last nine lines are separated by this assurance: "for you are with me." In the original Hebrew, both the first nine lines and the last nine lines contain exactly twenty-six words. And in the numerology of the ancient Hebrews, in which quantities were represented by letters of the alphabet, the number twenty-six would be expressed in the letters YHWH (Jehovah). Is that only a meaningless coincidence? Perhaps. But it might also hint at a most important fact: At the very center of our existence is God. And the central fact of a believer's life is that our God is a very present God. And the most important thing God wants us to know is that our God is with us. *With us.* Isaiah heard God saying to Israel, "When you pass through the waters, I will be with you" (Isaiah 43:2). And the seers of a thousand years looked forward to the coming of a Deliverer who would be called Emmanuel: *God with us.*

This realization, that God is with us–closer than hands and feet, nearer than thinking or breathing–is the point of transition in the psalm, as it is in life. We may face the rigors of passing through valleys of fear and darkness; we may be confronted by evils that threaten us; we may come to realize that the life of sheep in the wilderness isn't as tranquil and blissful as we may imagine. It may even occur to us, in those unguarded moments of existential panic, that death awaits us at the end of the path we travel. But when those circumstances of real life are filtered through the realization that "you are with me" (v. 4), those demons lose their threat.

For a fresh understanding of this psalm, try ending each line with the phrase "because God is with me!" Every cherished joy described in the psalm results from that one exhilarating realization. "I shall not want...I fear no evil...my cup overflows...I shall dwell in the house of the Lord...because God is with me!"

DAY 24
Read Psalm 24

The word *liturgy,* by which we refer to the prescribed ritual of a worship service, is derived from two Greek words: *Laos,* which means "people," and *ergon,* which means "work." Liturgy, then, is the work of the people. It is the people's participation in acts of glorifying God and seeking God's presence and blessing. Worship is not an exercise to be conducted only by the professional clergy. It is the work of the people.

Psalm 24 is a splendid example of the liturgy of the ancient Hebrew people. It was obviously composed for a specific experience of entrance. It was the introit that announced the beginning of worship. It was a celebration of the joy experienced by those who had walked many miles to enter the temple, and into the very presence of God, which the temple (and the tabernacle before it) symbolized.

One can easily see which lines of this psalm were sung by the worship leader and which were the responses of the people. It begins by reminding the worshipers that they are approaching no less a one than the Creator of all the universe. Coming into such a presence, then, deserves great solemnity and decorum. Surely those who blunder thoughtlessly and flippantly into such a presence are in violation of the holy dignity deserved by the object of our worship.

The conditions of entry into God's presence would seem to be rigid, indeed: clean hands, pure hearts, singleness of devotion to God. Who can pass such an entrance exam? The good news is that while our God deserves such reverent blamelessness in the lives of those who seek the holy presence, our Lord reaches out beyond the boundaries of our reverence to call those who could never qualify. The name of that good news is Jesus Christ.

As Jesus said to Zacchaeus, whose lifestyle would have immediately caused the guardians of the temple orthodoxy to reject his application for entrance, "'Today salvation has come to this house...for the Son of Man came to seek out and to save the lost'" (Luke 19:9–10). Jesus said those words on his way up to Jerusalem, where he was greeted by throngs of pilgrims who surely thought of this psalm as he entered through the Golden Gate: "Lift up your heads, O gates! and be lifted up, O ancient doors! that the King of glory may come in" (v. 7).

It is always a day of high celebration when Jesus, the King of glory and the seeker of lost souls, comes in—whether it is coming into a city or into a heart such as yours.

DAY 25
Read Psalm 25

If the psalms are poems (or hymns when set to music), in what way do they differ from prose? We are accustomed to poetry in which there is a pattern of meter or rhyme or some other conformity of expression. But these criteria seem to be absent in the psalms.

Where is the rhyme? Where is the cadence?

Part of the problem is that what we are reading in our Bibles is a translation of those poems, and what is clearly poetic in Hebrew often does not survive the transfer from one language to another. But there are some kinds of poetic construction that do make the trip from Hebrew to English without damage. One is the rhyming of phrases in which the same thought is repeated, but in different wording. For example:

> The law of the LORD is perfect, reviving the soul;
> The decrees of the LORD are sure, making wise the simple. (Psalm 19:7)

Sometimes the thought of the first line is not just repeated in the second, but carried forward to a logical conclusion:

> Happy are those
>   who do not follow the advice of the wicked,
> or take the path that sinners tread,
>   or sit in the seat of scoffers. (Psalm 1:1)

In this "progressive" rhyme of thought, the seriousness of the mistake of the wicked becomes more and more pronounced. Following the wrong advice is bad; choosing the path taken by sinners is worse; sitting down to "make oneself at home" among the scoffers expresses an intimacy and acceptance of evil that is the worst of the conditions.

Another type of poetry is the alphabetical acrostic, in which each succeeding line begins with the next letter of the Hebrew alphabet. The twenty-fifth Psalm is a splendid example of this kind of acrostic poem.

The theme of this psalm is teaching and learning, and that may be one of the reasons the psalmist carefully crafted this poem in such a way as to promote the learning of the Hebrew alphabet. Again and again through the psalm the writer pleads with God to teach the ways that would lead to an abundant life.

A teacher once boasted about having twenty-five years of teaching experience. One who knew the teacher's work well responded, "No, you have had one year's experience twenty-five times." The bridge between what we were yesterday and the better person we want to be tomorrow is education, whatever our age. And no one has the right to stop learning.

DAY 26
Read Psalm 26

At first glance this psalm seems to be an exercise in self-congratulation. The writer is unstinting in his depiction of himself as generous, faithful, innocent, and pure...not to mention humble! But we can forgive the psalmist a bit of boasting when we understand that he is pressed in some dangerous and life-threatening circumstance. His bill of particulars concerning his own rectitude is offered in much the same spirit as the testimony of the character witnesses brought into a trial: Can so virtuous a person possibly be deserving of punishment?

But God's favor is not purchased by our good deeds or exemplary character. Neither can it be said that our troubles always result from our sins and failures. To be sure, being good and doing good usually result in good fortune, while mistakes and sins have a notorious history of bringing hurt and sorrow on their perpetrators. But the psalmist knew full well–as did Jesus and Paul and a whole host of innocent sufferers in all the ages–that bad things do sometimes happen to good people. And sometimes evil people win the lottery or win a few skirmishes in the contest against righteousness. And if we expect to live as Christians, we'd better be prepared to find at times that the totally unmerited suffering of our savior finds at least some minor resemblance in our own experiences.

Some may ask, "If we're so Christian, how come we're not rich?" or immune to troubles, or spared any suffering or injustice? How can we hold onto faith when no immediate and practical benefit seems to result? How can we go on believing in God when God doesn't seem to be holding up the Lord's end of the bargain?

But believing in God when it is difficult to do so is when our faith means the most. Stand with Job at the mass grave of his family and hear him say, "The LORD gave, and the LORD has taken away; blessed be the name of the LORD" (Job 1:21). Hear Paul as he suffers a thorn in his side that he could neither remove nor endure, and hear him repeat God's message to him: "My grace is sufficient for you" (2 Corinthians 12:9). Hear Christ on the cross, crying out his anguish, "My God, my God, why have you forsaken me?" (Matthew 27:46). But also hear him say in valiant trust, "Into your hands I commend my spirit" (Luke 23:46).

Although our faith sometimes leads us through dark valleys, we know that God is with us. And in that knowledge, we can be at peace.

DAY 27
Read Psalm 27

The historic odyssey of the people of Israel leaving their place of bondage in Egypt in search of their own land is one of the most dramatic stories in the history of migration and resettlement. Some have conjectured that the rigors and difficulties they faced in their wilderness sojourn would have been made easier if they had known what lay ahead for them. But surely even the most stouthearted would have been turned back by such a premonition! The path that began in Egypt would lead them through forty years of hunger, deprivation, the blistering heat of the desert, the scourge of wild animals and poisonous snakes, the menace of ravenous desert tribes, the perpetual weariness of walking day after day, apparently without progress, to say nothing of their own rebellious discontent. The miracle is that even with such distractions, they stayed on track. What kept them going?

The secret came at the end of the first leg of their journey. According to Exodus 12, the first phase of their hike took them from Ramses, the capital of Egypt, through the Red Sea on dry land, to a pleasant village in the Midian plains named Succoth. There they found food and water, safety from their pursuers, and a place to rest.

Succoth came to represent the providential care of God, the sheltering presence of God where wounds are dressed, hungers are sated, weariness finds rest, and dangers may be forgotten. All along the way, in this heroic journey in the wilderness, God would be waiting for them in unexpected succoths, providing care and comfort.

It is this image that is frequently referred to in the psalms. "He will hide me in his shelter," (v. 5) uses the Hebrew name of the first such shelter, *sukkah,* to indicate such a secret place.

In celebration of all such divine shelters that the people of Israel had found through their history, a festival of succoths (or tabernacles or booths) became a regular annual celebration. By building such celebratory shelters out of branches and leaves and living in them for the week's observance, the people recalled how their ancestors—and all who trust God—have been provided places of rest, security, healing, and provender all along life's journey.

As you look forward to the future—either this one day, or for a lifetime ahead, or for all eternity—you cannot know what all you may be called on to face. But of this you may be absolutely certain: God will be there, too, and will provide you a place of safety, rest, and whatever resources you need to get you to the next succoth.

One of the reasons why so many people love the psalms is that many of these writings describe difficulties that are humanity's common lot. And in the course of the psalm, the writer works through distress, freely expressing fears and resentments. Then, in most cases, the psalm ends with an expression of victory over those vicissitudes—either a victory in fact or an assurance of triumph.

The book of Psalms has been called "The People's Bible" because these writings express common life problems with which all of us are painfully acquainted. A common formula for such psalms is to begin with a cry of despair and a complaint that God has turned a deaf ear to such grievances (such as Psalm 22:1, "My God, my God, why have you forsaken me?").

Then there follows a diatribe against the wicked, saying to God, "Those are the people who deserve such sufferings as you have given me! Why don't you punish them?"

But then, having expressed anguish and vented anger against those evildoers who deserve to be punished, the psalmist concludes with a ringing declaration of faith in the goodness of God.

Sometimes we are shocked by the depth of the resentment against God that the psalmist voices. But God is not offended by our honesty and would rather we reveal what we really are—warts and all—than to hide our genuine feelings behind pious phrases that dissemble rather than disclose. And perhaps it is not possible for us to see God clearly until our vision has been cleansed by the tears of suffering and sorrow.

So in this reading from "The People's Bible," we hear the writer struggling to face perilous circumstances as well as the danger of the loss of faith. And we hear outrage concerning the apparent ease of life enjoyed by the wicked. The psalmist calls on the Lord to exercise justice and punish those wrongdoers.

So having assessed the actual problems and having given expression to true feelings, the psalmist now comes back to a ringing affirmation of faith that has gone through the fires of doubt and emerged intact. "The LORD is the strength of his people," the psalmist says (v. 8). That is the conclusion that one draws not from tranquil study in an ivory tower, but in the throes of battle. And to honor such faith, the Lord will "be their shepherd, and carry them forever" (v. 9).

DAY 29
Read Psalm 29

Reading the psalms frequently delights the reader with such picturesque and graceful expressions that even when the meaning is obscure, the images adhere to the walls of memory and provide a mantra of beauty and grace. Such is the fragment in the sixth verse of the twenty-ninth Psalm that lilts, "He makes Lebanon skip like a calf" (v. 6). What a charming bucolic scene is dredged up by that picture! Life on the farm is basically a hardscrabble existence, demanding unrelenting labor and often small recompense. But there are flashes of humor and charm in the landscape of a farm, and a "skipping calf" is certainly one of them. There is humor in that snapshot of creation, and refreshment. The pragmatist would argue that such a sight is hardly an essential component in the operation of a farm. But watching a young calf celebrating its life in the awkward dance of existence gives us a glimpse into the mind and heart of the Creator.

This psalm, like Psalm 19, is an exercise in catching a glimpse of God by seeing the Divine reflected in creation. The "voice" of God is understood as the outreaching expression of God. It could also be thought of as the "word" of God. Either term expresses the belief that God is not aloof, not withdrawn from the earth and its family. Rather, the Creator dwells in the creation, ruling over the whole of it, demonstrating a power unmatched in the universe.

So God's voice may be heard in the rolling thunder, and in the mighty tides of the sea, and in the lightning that illuminates the night sky. As the Genesis hymn of creation says, "God said, 'Let there be light'; and there was light" (Genesis 1:3). So the voice of God says everything into existence, and the voice of God remains in control.

But sometimes that voice demonstrates not majesty and glory, but power and destructiveness. "The voice of the LORD breaks the cedars" (v. 5), which were the tallest and strongest trees the psalmist knew anything about. But even those towering monuments to God's might cannot withstand the power of God as demonstrated in the windstorms. Even those trees, in the control of the mighty God, dance in the storm and skip like a calf.

Does that mean that the cedars shiver and tremble and fall under the control of God? Or can it be said that knowing that our God has all things under ultimate control gives us the joyous abandon of newborn calves kicking up their heels in a dance of celebration? Perhaps it depends on what you are, and what you believe God is.

DAY 30
Read Psalm 30

Halford Luccock, the late professor of homiletics at Yale Divinity School, once confessed a great fondness for coconut macaroons. Early in his life he could hardly afford such delicacies, so he would buy only one or two, and they were quickly gone. He often longed for the time when he would be able to afford to buy the macaroons in quantity. But when the day came when his income would permit such an indulgence, he found that having a whole sack full of the treats diminished his appreciation of them. So he devised a plan to recapture the joy of a single macaroon: He hid each one in his study–some behind reference books, some in drawers in his desk, others in various places. And he would try to forget where they were. Then, when he happened upon one, it was like finding buried treasure, and once again he found delight in the unexpected macaroons.

Such an exercise in discovery and delight also attends our study of the psalms. Tucked into the writings, often in unexpected places, are some of the spiritual aphorisms that have become a part of the language. Such a literary gem is this sentence in the thirtieth Psalm: "Weeping may linger for the night, but joy comes with the morning" (v. 5). How many saints have leaned on that promise when passing through some dark night of the soul. And how many people have drawn sufficient comfort from its assurance to provide some rest in an otherwise restless night.

Our vocabulary is rich with allusions to the darkness as a symbol of evil. We say that "things are darkest just before the dawn," and "what is done in the dark cannot survive what is seen in the light." And no one who has ever suffered from insomnia can doubt the illusion that the minutes drag by on leaden feet during a sleepless night. But what comfort comes when the dark begins to yield its malevolence to the triumph of the sunrise!

For long centuries the prophets cried out their longing for the coming of God's messenger, saying, "Will not day come soon?" And Zechariah, John the Baptist's father, foretold the advent of the Messiah in the words, "The dawn from on high will break upon us, to give light to those who sit in darkness" (Luke 1:78–79).

Somehow we can endure the weeping that lingers through the long, dark night if we know that joy is coming in the morning. And those who have met the One whose death on Good Friday dissolved into joy on Easter can be sure that we too shall know the radiance of God's glory "when the morning breaks eternal bright and fair."

DAY 31
Read Psalm 31

Twice while Jesus was hanging on the cross he found a psalm to express the deep feelings he was experiencing in that time of extremity. Early in his ordeal he found words to express the emotions he surely felt, words from Psalm 22: "My God, my God, why have you forsaken me?" Though pain numbed his tongue and exhausted his strength so that he could not recite the entire psalm, surely his thoughts went beyond the cry of anguish in the first verse to a resolution of acceptance and peace, as expressed later in the psalm.

But once again, at the very end of his life, and standing forever as the last words he spoke in this life, is his quotation from Psalm 31: "Into your hand I commit my spirit" (v. 5). In the Greek language in which the New Testament was originally written, the word we translate "commit" is *paratheke*. It is a word used most often in commerce and banking matters, and is frequently translated "deposit." When we deposit something of value in a bank, we demonstrate great trust in that institution. Such a transaction requires us to let go of the treasure and put it in someone else's hands. But we are confident that we have not thereby lost the treasure or thrown it away or squandered it. We know that it still belongs to us and will one day be returned to us.

So Jesus' life was ebbing away. He had no possessions. The seamless robe, which was the only material asset he owned, had been gambled away by his executioners at the foot of the cross. Most of his followers had forsaken him and were in hiding. The new concept of a kingdom of heaven on earth, which had seemed just at the point of being realized, was now a forgotten dream. He had nothing to show for his sacrifice and dedication. All that was left was his life, and that was quickly ebbing away.

But there was one thing his adversaries could not claim as booty, and that was his soul. Beyond the reach of those executioners at the foot of the cross and the arrogant ecclesiastics who now relished their grisly victory, was the divine spirit that gave Jesus his nature, his character, his essence. And that treasure Jesus deposited into hands that were steady and strong, hands that would never let him go. "Into your hands I commit my spirit."

We all suffer losses that grieve us—the loss of health, or friends, or family, or money, or reputation. And all losses hurt. But what we put into God's hands is forever secure. And if that's where our heart is—and our spirit and our soul and our character and our hope—then no stock market crash, no physical infirmity, no perfidy of friends, or malevolence of foes, or calamity of chance can terrify us. God keeps watch over God's own.

DAY 32
Read Psalm 32

Not all bumper sticker axioms are to be trusted, but occasionally one finds truth even in that unlikely location. Such is the case with this confessional tidbit frequently seen in that automotive showcase: *"I'm not perfect—just forgiven."* As relieved as we may be to find a theological truth that can be packaged in so minimal a statement, there are some things to quibble about. First, perfection is not merely the absence of evil. Forgiveness wipes the slate of conscience clean, but perfection requires some positive ingredients. And being concerned about one's own perfection is a dead giveaway that such a blissful achievement has not yet been reached.

Nevertheless, there are some things to be said in favor of that bit of bumper sticker theology. First, it should occur to us that every one of us is in need of forgiveness. As the writer of First John points out, "If we say that we have no sin, we deceive ourselves, and the truth is not in us" (1 John 1:8). Even *after we have been forgiven,* our sinless state exists on borrowed time. Acknowledging our chronic human tendency toward sin is necessary if we are to be honest with ourselves, and honest with God.

And here is another inescapable truth: Unresolved sin endangers both the conscience and the eternal soul, and no peace is possible for those whose sin has not been dealt with. A cloud of remorse blocks out the radiance of joy as long as the sin remains to haunt us.

But the good news is that there is one who can dispose of our sin, and that is God, who finds great delight in providing that service. Listen to the extravagant language the Bible uses to express this ministry of God:

> For as the heavens are high above the earth,
>   so great is his steadfast love toward those who fear him;
> as far as the east is from the west,
>   so far he removes our transgressions from us. (Psalm 103:11–12)

What a relief for those who have been burdened by their feelings of guilt and despair. And it is not because of what we are or what we do that God provides this cleansing. It is because of what God is and what God has done through Christ. Happy, indeed, are those whose transgression is forgiven, whose sin is covered.

DAY 33
Read Psalm 33

In the decade of the 1960s many congregations were torn asunder by the controversy over whether guitars had a rightful place in the worship of God. And a century before, the same sort of ecclesiastical squabbles were waged over the validity of pipe organs in church. And hand-clapping and shouting have been seen by some as valid expressions of joyful praise and by others as meaningless noise. The current debate is focused on "contemporary" or "traditional" worship, and hundreds of congregations have discovered a truth that should have been recognized earlier: People are different!

If anyone is looking for scriptural authorization for any style or medium of worship, the evidence is not hard to find. Like the apostle Paul, who condemned "speaking in tongues" in one phrase, then condoned it in the next sentence, the church has had to concede that in the vast repertoire of human experience, there is an almost unlimited catalog of components that may be used in the service of divine praise.

Psalm 33 provides a veritable index of such makings for worship. What about musical instruments? "Praise the LORD with the lyre," the psalmist says, and "play skillfully on the strings." What about contemporary songs? "Sing to him a new song," we are instructed. And what about those shouted praises? Rejoice "with loud shouts," the writer instructs (vv. 2–3).

And what of those who claim that real worship and service to God must be found in pursuing ministries of peace and justice? "All his work is done in faithfulness," this worship instruction continues, "He loves righteousness and justice" (vv. 4–5).

And what of those who seek to express their reverence in silence? "Let all the inhabitants of the world stand in awe of him," we are told (v. 8).

The fact is that God is not hard to please when we offer God our sincere praise and present ourselves in service. But there is a social responsibility in our worship as well. What we do to honor God must be a witness to others and a demonstration of our concern for them. And our expressions of praise must be as beautiful and as inspiring to others as they are satisfying to us. (Remember that the psalmist instructed us to play *skillfully*.)

Above all, it should be remembered that the word *worship* comes from the old English "worth-ship,"–that is, something that honors the worth of God. Therefore, what we render to God must be our best.

DAY 34
Read Psalm 34

There is an unsolvable mystery in the introduction of Psalm 34: "Of David, when he feigned madness before Abimelech, so that he drove him out, and he went away." There are four minor characters in the Old Testament who share the name Abimelech, but not one of them figures prominently in any story of David's life. So the fragment of truth preserved in the prologue raises several questions. What was the danger or difficulty that confronted David? And what had he done to get himself in such a fix? (We like to think that our heroes are always innocent of wrongdoing and that any difficulty they face results from the evil of their adversaries.) And since David was known to have been successful in resorting to violence in defeating his enemies, what prompted his subterfuge? And why would madness–either feigned or genuine–cause Abimelech to send him away?

To those questions, we shall probably never find answers. But the essence of the prologue is that David was in the throes of some predicament that involved both danger and difficulty, and he was able to find a way out of his problem. For that resolution, he was grateful to God. But that begs the question: Why was he grateful to God? Why not boast of his own cleverness and skill? Perhaps, and here is where we must read between the lines, David spent lonely and frightening hours or days–as a prisoner threatened with execution–in prayer and communion with God.

In the catalog of Christian martyrs is the story of a Christian who was condemned to death because of his faith. He was thrown into a dungeon and informed that at sunrise the next day he would be burned at the stake. That night in his lonely cell, he prayed, "Lord, give me grace to bear the fire! Please, Lord, give me grace to bear the fire!" But the voice of God came to him saying, "No, today I give you grace to bear the fear. Tomorrow I will give you grace to bear the fire."

So God gave David grace to bear the fear. And in that time of communion with God, as David awaited his execution, he found within his own mind the idea that would be his salvation and the mental resources to accomplish the feat.

Isn't it amazing how much smarter we are when we have spent some time with God in prayer? What good ideas occur to us, and what lavish resources with which to make our God-given ideas become realities.

As the poet said: "We kneel, how weak; we rise, how full of power!" And it was in celebration of that kind of empowerment that David wrote this psalm of praise and gratitude.

In 1787, fifty-five representatives of the American colonies met in Philadelphia to draft our Constitution, which would guide the destiny of our country. Thomas Jefferson was appointed chairman of a subcommittee charged with the responsibility of bringing before the convention a proposal on slavery to become a part of the Constitution. Jefferson labored over a carefully worded statement that would have forever prohibited human bondage in the United States from its very beginning. The committee pondered the proposal, debated it, and finally voted on it. Sentiment on the committee was evenly divided, but at the very last moment one man, who held the tie-breaking vote, made the decision. And he voted to reject Jefferson's proposal, thus permitting slavery in this country.

Jefferson, who could foresee the suffering and anguish that would inevitably result from this tacit approval of so dehumanizing an institution as slavery, later reported that breathless moment when the deciding vote was cast. He wrote, "And heaven was silent in that awful moment."

The writer of Psalm 35 was agonizing over another such moment, one in his own life, in which he had longed to hear some comforting or strengthening word from heaven, but "heaven was silent." And we have all suffered through those human experiences in which we pounded with raw and bleeding knuckles on the gate of heaven in our most fervent prayers, but received no reply except the hollow echo of our own laments.

A heartbroken mother had watched helplessly as her teenaged son died from injuries suffered in an automobile accident. All her prayers could not seem to bring any beneficial result. She asked her pastor, with some resentment, "Where was God when my son was killed?" The pastor replied gently, "God was where God was when God's own son was killed: just beyond the horizon preparing the joy of Easter."

Beloved of God, be assured that God knows you, knows what you are going through, and cares. And God's presence with you, as you go through your dark valleys, will bring you to the joy and victory of a new day.

DAY 36
Read Psalm 36

This lovely writing provides a classic pattern by which many of the psalms are constructed. At the beginning is the ailment or dilemma. It is a common illness known to all human beings: sin. The wicked person has rejected wisdom and conscience, and in idleness the person plots and plans new ways to demonstrate rebellion against the will of God. So callous has the rebel's soul become that even the thought of God does not stir any feelings of remorse for wickedness. In stubborn rejection of God's authority, the person has taken a step beyond the point of no return. There is no hope for this deliberate scofflaw...except for one thing: the love of God.

The second element in this pattern is the remedy for even the most hopelessly sinsick soul. It is the amazing grace of a God who still claims us as children, even long after we have rejected God as a loving parent. Like the father in Jesus' parable of the prodigal son, God keeps watching that road back home for any sign of the returning wanderer, eager to throw all divine dignity to the winds in careless abandon, to lavish divine love upon one who does not begin to deserve it.

So beautiful is this astonishing love of God that the psalmist employs several lovely visions to hint at its magnificence: the shadow of your wings, the abundance of your house, the river of delight, and the fountain of life. In fact, the love of God seems to be the magic bullet that conquers all evil. Except for one thing: It doesn't work if it isn't applied.

The third stage of this pattern indicates that no matter how powerful the love of God in conquering evil, it is powerless until it permeates the life of a person. Even the most potent medicines are ineffective as long as they stay in the bottle or the medicine chest.

"Continue your steadfast love to those who know you," the psalmist prays (v. 10). And knowing God implies walking with God and fulfilling God's wisdom in our obedience.

In other words: "No God, no peace; know God, know peace."

DAY 37
Read Psalm 37

Here is one of only two psalms in which the writer's age is identified. "I have been young, and now am old"(v. 25), the psalmist writes. (The other, in which the author begs God not to forsake him in his old age, is Psalm 71.)

A second thing to note about this psalm is that, like several others (such as Psalms 25 and 34, which we have already seen), this is an acrostic poem, with the first letter of the first Hebrew word of every other line following the Hebrew alphabet. This was undoubtedly an aid to memory, since the psalms were meant to be memorized for use in public worship as well as in private devotion. And having such a "hook" to hang the lines of the poem on would aid the worshiper in recalling the words.

But aside from such superficial observations, there is an undeniable charm to this psalm, for it represents the homely conclusions of a person of faith after a lifetime of learning by living. "I have been young, and now am old, yet I have not seen the righteous forsaken or their children begging bread" (v. 25). Such a conclusion about God's providential care of those who live righteous lives was not drawn from theological deductions, but from long years of experience. Note that the psalmist does not claim that there was never a righteous person forsaken nor that there were never any children of the righteous who were reduced to begging. Such may indeed have existed. But the psalmist says only that "I have not seen" such tragedies.

And while the great eternal truths may not be within the reach of our experiences, by the time we have lived with God for a long lifetime, what we have seen ought to be enough to go on.

Long years of experience with the Christian faith also gives us a certain amount of patience and endurance, so that we need not "fret ourselves" because of evildoers. God does not have to settle all accounts by Saturday evening for us to continue to trust the Lord of all creation.

Again and again, through this homely, practical, and reassuring psalm, we see that walking in the path of God yields enough evidence, along the way, that what we have seen of God is reasonable encouragement to trust God for all that we have not seen.

DAY 38
Read Psalm 38

Modern counselors are fond of reminding us that the word *emotion* means, in its root form, "a moving out," and indicates that expressing our emotions is like moving out of our system the bitterness or hatred or guilt that festers in our innermost being. When we keep our emotions bottled up, we are hoarding poison.

No one could accuse the psalmist of bottling up emotions in this psalm! And if "confession is good for the soul," the writer must have had a most healthy soul, indeed, after this full disclosure of faults, sins, and troubles.

Although we are not aware of many of David's sins, we do know of his immoral dalliance with Bathsheba and his subsequent plot to have her husband, Uriah, killed in battle to keep his sin from becoming known. But David appeared to be uncommonly conscious of his own wrongdoings and frequently gave voice to them. "My sin is ever before me," he said in Psalm 51:3.

But despite this apparent preoccupation with his sin, David was also quick to acknowledge God's love for him. "Guard me as the apple of the eye" (17:8). Here is one of the mysteries of the Christian faith: that God, who is perfect, and utterly and unrelentingly opposed to evil, can also be so accepting and loving toward one who freely acknowledges a sinful nature. Our familiar admonition to "hate the sin, but love the sinner" could aptly be spoken of God's attitude, for as paradoxical as it may seem, that is precisely what God does.

But not all our sorrows result from our iniquities. Sometimes, as the psalmist acknowledges, there are those who, without cause, hurt us intentionally. At other times, we fall because our "foot slips" (v. 16).

Whatever their cause, human hurts give us pain, and, as the old saying puts it, "when something hurts, God helps." The great prayer by Saint Francis of Assisi says, "Where there is injury, let me sow pardon." Occasionally someone objects to this line. Shouldn't it have said, "Where there is injury, let me sow *healing*"? But perhaps David knew, and Francis knew, what God wants us to know: that at the root of all our hurts is sin—someone's sin, usually our own. And when we are injured, it is God's pardon that we need and that God will freely give.

DAY 39
Read Psalm 39

An American churchwoman was touring India and, while there, decided to look up the missionary that her church had supported through outreach offerings. She found him at his home—a small, cheerless house with no windows and almost entirely devoid of furniture. She could not help but ask the dedicated man of God, "But where is your furniture?" In reply the missionary turned the question back to her: "Where is *your* furniture?" "But I'm only passing through," the woman protested. The missionary replied, "And so am I."

How much less important the "furniture" of life seems when we put it in the context of the brief sojourn of our earthly visit.

The psalmist expresses this perspective in the lovely thirty-ninth Psalm, in which the writer confesses, "I am your passing guest, an alien, like all my forebears" (v. 12). The three words "*your passing guest*" hold a multitude of truths that should free us from anxiety and release us from materialism. The word *your* reminds us that the space and time of our earthly visit belong to God, and we are here at God's invitation. Like a careful and conscientious host, God provides a place for us and a time in which to spend our days, though both place and time are God's. We cannot cling to either our space or our time (or the toys we have accumulated by the expenditure of our space and time) because they belong to God and will be ours only as long as it pleases God to allow them to be so.

But we are *passing* guests, which means that we cannot cling to our present opportunities and resources. Like a puff of smoke, or like a shadow, our lives are fragile and ephemeral. Such a realization might be something to mourn, except for the fact that "My hope is in you" (v. 7).

We are *guests* of the almighty God. The momentary finds its hope in the eternal. And we do not come to the eternal God as beggars, impertinently importuning our host for security that we cannot achieve through our own accomplishments. We come to God knowing that God has invited us, *as guests* to live in the house and eat of the food that God provides for guests.

So the passing becomes the permanent, and the evanescent becomes the eternal, when we realize who we are and who God is.

DAY 40

In Nottingham, England, is the Wesleyan Chapel where William Booth, founder of the Salvation Army, was converted. A memorial tablet marks the spot where this notable friend of the friendless received his baptism of spiritual power and purpose. Salvation Army leaders from around the world journey to that chapel as to a shrine. One day an aged man in the uniform of the Army was found by the minister of the chapel, standing with uplifted eyes before the tablet.

"Can a man say his prayers here?" he asked. "Of course," was the minister's reply, "a man can say his prayers here." The old Salvation Army officer went down on his knees and, lifting his hands before the tablet, he prayed, "O God, do it again! Do it again."

Surely it was not too much to ask of God to do what God had, on at least one occasion, done in another context. As the hymn "Great Is Thy Faithfulness" says to God, "as thou hast been thou forever wilt be." Or as James expresses the truth in his epistle, "(in God) there is no variation or shadow due to change" (James 1:17). As perfidious and inconstant as we may be in our dealings with God, God does not condescend to mirroring our faults.

The scenario that prompted the writing of this psalm appears to be this: David had experienced some frightening and dangerous adversity, in which he felt trapped like a prisoner behind bars. But he appealed to God, who came to his rescue. And unlike many people who pray arduously for some divine favor, but never think of returning to God with some expression of thanks for the blessing, David witnessed to this saving blessing before the whole congregation. He credited God with his victory and offered his life as an obedient tool in God's hands, to help accomplish the divine will.

But unfortunately, misfortune has more lives than a junkyard cat, and no sooner had David expressed his thanks for deliverance from that prior difficulty than he found himself once again trapped in some adversity, which brought him back to God, saying, "O Lord, do it again!"

And the wonder is that God never tires of hearing such prayers. Nothing pleases God more than being given the opportunity to fulfill the holy prerogative of answering prayers. The problem is that we so seldom bring to God a vessel for putting such a blessing in. And that vessel is a yielded life.

DAY 41
Read Psalm 41

This psalm is generally considered to be the last of the first book of psalms, and there are evidences that the original compiler of the psalms intended such an arrangement. For example, there is a closing ascription: "Blessed be the LORD, the God of Israel, from everlasting to everlasting. Amen and Amen" (v. 13). Clearly that was intended as a final blessing, not unlike the benedictions with which the New Testament epistles end. The Talmud suggests that "as Moses gave five books of laws to Israel, so David gave five books of psalms to Israel."

But there is another striking clue that Psalm 41 was intended as a finale to the first book of psalms: It is an echo of the first psalm. Like bookends, the first and the forty-first psalms show similarities and differences, and between the two they contain the full range of Old Testament thought.

Think of the first line of each of the psalms: "Happy are those," begins the first psalm, and so echoes the forty-first. But in their very similarity is their difference. For Psalm 1 teaches that happiness may be found in one's own personal character and piety. But Psalm 41 teaches that real happiness must be found in sensitivity and service to the poor, the powerless, and the suffering. "Happy are those who consider the poor" (v. 1).

Surely more than "considering" is necessary. But the Hebrew word thus translated has the deeper meaning of "giving attention to" or "focusing on." The clear teaching here is that active concern for the powerless is a necessary aspect of the character of the man or woman of faith.

And the implication here is that such a concern for the poor results in God's favor given both to the poor and to the one who has concern for such unfortunate people. Here is a mature conviction that would seem more at home in the pages of the gospels than in the psalms. But as Jesus would later say in many different ways, when we allow ourselves to be instruments of God's blessing, we both give and receive the kindness of God.

DAY 42
Read Psalm 42

Many scholars believe that Psalms 42 and 43 were once a single psalm that somehow got separated in the compiling process. One reason for this belief is the fact that the same refrain is repeated several times in both psalms: "Why are you cast down, O my soul, and why are you disquieted within me?"

It is, as the King of Siam would say, "a puzzlement!" As the psalmist reported, so could we also affirm that we have had adequate experience with the living God to be assured of God's providential care for us in the present and in the future. There are a multitude of reasons that we should never be dispirited. But still the times of depression come. A favorite hymn ("His Eye Is on the Sparrow") seems, like the psalmist, almost obsessed with the oxymoron phrase, "a sad Christian." It says:

> Why should I feel discouraged? Why should the shadows come?
> Why should my heart be lonely, and long for heaven and home?

But the very fact that both the psalmist and the hymn writer (Civilla D. Martin) describe the condition so clearly, in words that resonate in our own hearts, gives evidence that such a tragedy is common among us. Why should we feel discouraged when we have the promises of a God who has never failed us nor forsaken us?

Perhaps what we interpret as discouragement is really the last, clinging grasp of doubt that won't quite let us give ourselves completely to God. There is always a "what if" that dangles over our heads and attaches footnotes of gloom to our doxologies. Even John the Baptist had his despondency, and the Lord of all life agonized on the cross with a heartrending expression of fleeting doubt, "My God, my God, why hast thou forsaken me?"

The truth is that faith must always be faith and can never—this side of heaven—become fact. A blind, reckless, ungrounded leap of faith has to brave the vacuum that stretches between the known and the unknowable.

But joy is a fruit of the spirit, according to Paul (Galatians 5:22). Joy is produced by the Spirit of God within us. It is the song that rises from a broken heart, the flower that springs from the blood-soaked soil of a battlefield. And it is not only the privilege but also the duty of a Christian to be joyful.

DAY 43

"Send out your light and your truth; let them lead me" (v. 3). So the psalmist beseeches God in a time of discouragement and despondency. "Let them bring me to your holy hill and to your dwelling." One of America's great universities has as its motto "*Lux et Veritas,*" a Latin phrase that also identifies these two changeless entities. But unlike those who think of biblical faith as a matter of chasing flickering shadows and blindly accepting baseless presumptions, the psalmist understands that any discovery of light or obedience to truth will lead us directly to God. The person of faith has nothing to fear from science or myth. Any search for truth brings us closer to God.

"You will know the truth, and the truth will make you free," Jesus said (John 8:32). He did not invite his followers to ignore the truth or to shield their eyes from the light. He challenged them to think their purest thoughts and obey their most transparently good instincts, to follow them faithfully, and they would find themselves at the end of it all in the presence of God. And that truth would give them freedom from fear, from meaninglessness, and from despair. The truth would lead them.

Light and truth are, therefore, holy allies of those who seek God. But ironically, light and truth are staunch enemies of those who pursue evil. A light suddenly turned on in a room that has been neglected will quickly reveal dust and chaos. The correct answers to a final quiz will cruelly expose inadequate preparation and study. It is not a vindictive God who judges and condemns our carelessness, but our own failure to seek the real light and the honest truth.

From time to time some Christians and some scientists engage in a heated debate about which discipline is more useful in discovering the truth. But there is no conflict between science and religion: Both are attempts to discover the truth. Like mountain climbers who seek to climb the same peak but start at different points around its base, scientists and people of faith are seeking the same light and truth, and the closer they come to their ultimate goal, the closer they will be to each other.

Whether we are in a chemical laboratory or in a study of the scriptures, God invites us to seek, discover, and obey the light we glimpse and the truth we learn.

DAY 44
Read Psalm 44

It is not uncommon for Christian people to long for "the good old days" when the people of faith enjoyed the magnificent blessing of God, and everything seemed to be "coming up roses." But such days are hard to recognize when we are passing through them. It is only when we wear the rose-colored glasses of memory that we can discern the halcyon days of glory.

Ask any Jewish person when the "good old days" of Jewish history were experienced, and the person will likely identify the era of David's reign as that sublime age. If you had asked contemporaries of Jesus, they also would have pointed proudly to the time when David was king. Their messianic hope was focused on the possibility that another David would occupy the throne of Israel. On Palm Sunday, Jesus' entrance into the Holy City was accompanied by the paeans of praise that begged God for a return to the "good old days" of the "kingdom of our ancestor David" (Mark 11:10).

But note this: it was in that remembered time–so cherished as the golden age of Israel–that the psalmist poured out this lament, identifying the age in which he lived as a time when Israel was a laughingstock of the nations. The psalmist was still looking backward to a previous golden age, when God had visited the people and given them victory piled on victory.

Also note this: it was when the people of Jerusalem were longing for a past halcyon age that a carpenter from Nazareth was among them, teaching them God's truth and inviting them to become participants in God's new kingdom. What a joy it should have been for those people who saw Jesus and heard his teachings. But they were unable to see the glorious possibilities of the days in which they lived. Their eyes were blinded by the magnificent splendor of the past.

It is always a mistake to assume that God is either incapable or unwilling to make any time "the good new days." The psalmist was a bit later to declare that God is "a very present help in trouble" (Psalm 46:1). How present is *very* present? God is undeniably, gloriously, reliably present in every moment and circumstance of your life.

Whether your days are "good new days" or not depends on your response to that glorious truth.

DAY 45
Read Psalm 45

Despite the avalanche of peripherals—such as candles, flowers, music, and the protocols that mandate who sits where—a wedding can be one of life's most beautiful customs. It is a ceremony that crosses cultural, racial, and religious boundaries and is as ubiquitous as the love between a man and a woman that calls for such a celebration. Every participant is scrubbed and shining for the big moment, and nowhere is there a hint of the pains and troubles that will surely come in the life to be shared by the happy couple.

The Jewish ceremony has a custom that adds a sobering note to the blissful milieu. A crystal goblet (wrapped in a napkin to guard against injury) is stepped on and broken by the groom. Although originally intended as a recollection of the destruction of the temple, the sound of glass breaking is a reminder of the brokenness and resulting injury and pain that are ever-present possibilities in a marriage. In all the days after the strains of Wagner and Mendelssohn have been forgotten, that sound of breaking crystal will still echo through the marriage.

Psalm 45 is a wedding psalm, which was written as a special occasion song to be sung at a royal wedding. So beautiful are its phrasing and its depictions of the happy bridegroom and the gracious bride that in all the centuries since it was written, this psalm has been a favorite scripture to be read or sung at a Jewish wedding. It was clearly written to be used at a royal wedding. The king himself is the groom, and he is extolled as handsome, brave, pure, and just, enjoying the faithful allegiance of his subjects.

Likewise, the bride is described in glowing terms. She and her bridesmaids in their magnificent array provide an enchanting processional into the palace of the king. What could possibly happen to spoil the promise of such a day?

Unfortunately, this wedding psalm was written for the nuptials of the spineless King Ahab and his treacherous queen, Jezebel. Do you hear the crystal being shattered in that ceremony?

Everything good must have a start somewhere; likewise, everything bad has a beginning. But while a good beginning is beneficial, and a bad start can be overcome, the worth of any endeavor will be realized in the long desert stretches that extend tediously between beginning and end, when the sound of breaking crystal provides the background music.

DAY 46
Read Psalm 46

A recent cartoon depicted Adam and Eve as they left the Garden of Eden after their expulsion from that idyllic place. Both have expressions of confusion and dejection on their faces, as Adam says to his spouse, "My dear, we are living in a time of transition." And so it has been in every succeeding generation. Every age is an age of change, and change is always uncomfortable and sometimes painful. So the psalmist says, "We are living in a time of transition." And the convulsive changes are cataclysmic and frightening. An earthquake shatters all the familiar landmarks. Familiar sources of strength are toppling. The security of their beloved nation is threatened. Neighboring nations become foes instead of allies.

But to the citizens of Jerusalem there is a promise of shelter from such alarms. Their city is also the City of God, the Holy City, the very residence of the Supreme! And as suggested by their very topography, they have the high privilege of living on an elevated plateau. From their lofty vantage point they can watch for invaders and dispatch them. And since God is in heaven, they are closer to God than are the valley dwellers. God is both their shelter (refuge) when attacked and their fortress (strength) when they attack.

But in the midst of all these fireworks and traumas, God gets a word in edgewise. "Be still!" God commands, "and know that I am God" (v. 10). The Hebrew word we translate "be still" means, in its root form, "give place" or "make room." An ancient prayer beseeches God, "O Lord, today I have many things to do and will be very busy. And if I should forget you, Lord, please don't forget me!"

Well, we needn't worry about that! God will never forget us. We are engraved on God's heart. But when in the press of business we leave no room for God, we deprive ourselves of the quiet oasis of strength and encouragement that communion with God always provides. If you are too busy to pray, you are too busy!

DAY 47
Read Psalm 47

It is said that when Sir Christopher Wren completed the construction of St. Paul's Cathedral in London, he proudly showed the finished product to a friend. At the conclusion of the tour, the guest, who had been silent throughout the exercise, said to his host, "I find it awful and artificial." And Sir Christopher was overjoyed! In that time, of course, "awful" meant "inspiring awe," and artificial meant "artistic."

So when the psalmist proclaims that "the LORD, the Most High, is terrible" (v. 2, RSV), it means that our God is a Lord of astonishing power. In fact, we might say—as a contemporary Christian song puts it—"Our God is an awesome God!"

The ancient Hebrew people had a legend that God sent two angels to earth every day to collect the prayers of the people. One angel was to collect the prayers of petition, in which people sought God's help. The other angel was given the happy task of gathering up all the prayers of praise and thanksgiving. At the end of the day the "petition" angel returned to heaven with back bowed by the heavy burden of requests. But the "praise" angel had collected so few prayers of thanksgiving that this angel lent assistance to the other. This should remind us that even when our praises do not seem nearly as urgent as our "asking" prayers, the praises frequently offer surprising help with our needs.

Psalm 47 is a splendid example of a praise psalm. No request is made of God, no petulant complaint that God has failed to perform as expected, no cry of despair because God has not been as prompt in distributing blessings as the people might wish. There is only a celebration of the greatness and goodness of an awesome God. And how it must have delighted God to hear it, and how it must have lightened the hearts of God's people to sing it!

After the ascension of Jesus, the disciples were left with an enormous responsibility. "Go therefore and make disciples of all nations," Jesus had charged them (Matthew 28:19). Surely they must get busy! There was not a moment to lose! There was so much to do. But the gospel of Luke ends with a most telling thought: "And they were continually in the temple blessing God" (Luke 24:53). A waste of time? Ah, no! It was in the temple that they found the direction and the strength to go into all the world. And it was in their blessing God that they achieved the focus of their faith that gave them the message that they were take to the uttermost parts of the earth.

DAY 48
Read Psalm 48

Anyone who has ever attempted to explain spiritual truths in terms of material understandings can have sympathy for the pastor of a small church. He had been asked by the teacher of a Sunday school class of kindergartners to tell them the story of Jesus' ascension and to explain its meaning. To aid him in his presentation, the pastor had brought a large, life-size picture of Jesus into the classroom. Step-by-step he attempted to lead the children to discover the answer to the question of where Jesus is now. "If Jesus walks on your feet," he asked, "and works with your hands, and hears through your ears, and looks out at the world through your eyes, where you do suppose Jesus lives now?" The children rewarded the pastor with the expected answer: "Jesus lives inside us," they chorused triumphantly. That seemed to satisfy all the children except for one. Timmy was sitting over in a corner of the room, and his mental processes could be assumed as he studied that large picture of Jesus. "But he's so big, and I'm so small," his reasoning must have gone. "How can that big man live inside me?" Finally he burst out, "If Jesus lives inside me, it seems to me he ought to stick out somewhere!"

Congratulations, Timmy! You put your finger on a truth that has been missed by many people through the centuries. Like those people of the psalmist's time who kept thinking that God was confined to the city of Jerusalem and its hilly precincts, many have missed the meaning of God's message to Jonah, that God is everywhere a human being can be. To be sure, God had revealed divine power and truth in that location of the temple. The very stones had taken on a patina of glory because of the heroism and faith of God's people. God was present in the Holy City, to be sure. But God was also present in the desert, where Jesus met the tempter and came out of the experience cleansed and focused. And God was on the little hill just outside the city gate, where God's son offered the willing sacrifice of his life for the redemption of the world.

And God is present in every church, where the godliest of men and women have given their blood, toil, sweat, and tears to make the presence of Christ known. And God is in every life experience in which God's presence is sought, revered, and obeyed.

And if God is in you, shouldn't God stick out somewhere?

DAY 49
Read Psalm 49

The psalmist goes to great lengths to make it clear that the warnings in this psalm are applicable to all people: "low and high, rich and poor." We all have a tendency to suppose that the stern warnings of scripture are meant for people other than ourselves. That is particularly so when the warnings have to do with material possessions and our reliance on them. We hear Jesus' teaching, "What will it profit them to gain the whole world and forfeit their life?" (Mark 8:36). And we sigh in relief and say, "Well, there's no danger that I'll ever gain the whole world!" Or we read the words in this psalm that warn against putting our trust in material goods, and we say, "Well, that's one thing poor folks like me never have to worry about!" As Tevye said in *Fiddler on the Roof,* "Being poor may not be a disgrace, but it's no great honor either!" Many people stubbornly cling to the illusion that there is a kind of honor in being poor, that at least if they are poor, materialism is not a danger for them! But poverty does not make us immune to materialism. It isn't what we have that determines our character, but what *has us.*

But whether we are rich or poor, we are still faced with the challenge of finding something to build our lives on that will not fail us. We simply must accept the fact that, as the psalm warns us, we cannot ransom ourselves (v. 7). We cannot save ourselves. We cannot raise ourselves from the dead.

A short story related the sad experience of a rich society dowager who took an ocean cruise. In order to impress the other passengers, she brought along her glittering collection of diamond jewelry. Shortly after she checked into her stateroom, the steward knocked on her door and asked if she would like to put her jewelry in the safe in the bursar's office. She declined, explaining, with some condescension, that she had already placed her gems in the wall safe in her stateroom. The attendant tried to explain that there was no wall safe in her room. She triumphantly pointed to the round door in the wall of her room. It was a porthole!

Where are you putting your valuables—especially your expendable treasures of time, effort, ability, and allegiance? Are they safe where you are depositing them?

DAY 50
Read Psalm 50

What can you give to someone who has everything? That is a frequently asked question in these affluent days. Shopping for a birthday or Christmas present for someone who doesn't really need anything is a difficult chore. As a result, billions of dollars are spent every holiday as people buy baubles and doodads in the hope that the intended recipients will find some pleasure in such trophies of affluence.

How much more difficult, then, to find a gift to give God, who really does have everything. "The cattle on a thousand hills" are God's, the psalm reminds us (v. 10). And all the birds in the air and the beasts in the forest are God's. What makes us think we can offer an animal slain on the altar as a gift that God will accept with joy? (It is interesting that despite the teachings in this psalm and in other places in the Old Testament that express God's disgust with animal sacrifices, the grisly practice continued until the temple was destroyed in 70 C.E.)

But God does want something from us—an honest acknowledgement of how God has blessed us. A simple gesture that says thank you to God is all that is required. But coming into God's presence, even to deliver a message of thanks, must surely make us aware of our sinfulness and our need of forgiveness, so before we can say thank you, we must first say, "I'm sorry." "The sacrifice acceptable to God is a broken spirit; a broken and contrite heart, O God, you will not despise" (Psalm 51:17).

And the reason God wants our contrition and our thanksgiving is not because these gifts will make God any richer, but because God wants the effect of those spiritual exercises in our own souls. We cannot go blundering arrogantly into the presence of God. There must be some recognition of who God is, and of how little we deserve to be in that holy presence, before we will have eyes to see the eternal glory. And if in our poverty of spirit we see God, there will surely result from that experience an expression of thanksgiving that will well up from the depths of our souls and spill over in joyous praise.

And those are the only appropriate gifts for the God who has everything.

DAY 51
Read Psalm 51

Most of the psalms leave us guessing about the circumstances or events or realizations that prompted their writing. But there is no need to guess in the case of the fifty-first psalm. The occasion is clearly identified in the heading to the psalm, which says, "A Psalm of David, when the prophet Nathan came to him, after he had gone in to Bathsheba." Everyone knows the tawdry story of David's moral collapse, which involved the seduction of a young married woman and the murder of her husband, Uriah, in an attempt to hide David's sin. Knowing everything else we know about David, we can only ask, "What got into him? What made him do it?"

The truth is that no one is ever immune to temptation. Even Jesus was tempted in every respect, as we are (Hebrews 4:15). And while Jesus was able to withstand the snares of the tempter, it was with great difficulty and agony that such a victory was won. We dare not judge David too harshly, for it might be a case of the pot calling the kettle black.

And we are shocked to learn that apparently David was able to live with his guilt until he learned that somebody else knew about it. Nathan the prophet, acting on God's behalf, accused David of his sin. It was then that David realized his need of forgiveness.

The whole psalm is an expression of David's repentance and his experience of forgiveness and renewal. But it should be pointed out that David's restoration could not completely wipe out the effects of his sin. Uriah was still dead. Bathsheba was pregnant with the child of David's adultery. And David himself, like Jacob after his night of wrestling with the presence of God at the ford of the Jabbok, was a different person. Perhaps he was a bit less judgmental of others whose sins were exposed. Perhaps he was a bit less confident of his own ability to withstand temptation. Surely God's forgiveness must be understood as a gift with strings attached.

W. H. Auden wrote, "The world is admirably arranged: I love to sin, and God loves to forgive." And thus, he dismissed blithely any thought of the cost of forgiveness, or the necessity of some resulting change in the character of the one forgiven.

How was David changed by this experience? He had a new purpose in life: "Then I will teach transgressors your ways, and sinners will return to you" (v. 13). Such a resolution was the expression of David's joy over having been forgiven and restored.

Some things we learn better in times of distress and failure than in periods of prosperity and happiness. Even remorse over our guilt has important lessons to teach us.

DAY 52
Read Psalm 52

The heading identifies this psalm as "A Maskil of David." A maskil (sometimes spelled "masquil") was a set of instructions, or a homily. We are also informed in the heading that the occasion of the psalm was a time when David was being pursued by the tyrant king, Saul. David sought sanctuary in the tabernacle at Nob and obtained food there. When word of this assistance David received in the tabernacle reached the ears of King Saul, the monarch was so enraged that he ordered the massacre of many of the priests and others who lived near the tabernacle. More than eighty-five people were eventually killed to satisfy Saul's rage.

How this tragedy must have haunted David. Though he was essentially guiltless, it was nevertheless because of David that many people were killed. How could David live with his conscience?

It was to express his grief and anger over Saul's vengeful act that David wrote this teaching psalm. Saul was the "mighty one" who was guilty of the mischief done against the godly. "You love evil more than good," David charged him (v. 3). But David warned Saul that his sin would backfire. "God will break you down forever…he will uproot you from the land of the living" (v. 5).

This is an unhappy psalm, born in a time of cruelty and tragedy. But the homily David preaches from this experience is that Saul will not get away with it. He will pay the price for such evil. David believed in a just universe in which every sin is punished and every good deed rewarded. And David believed in the eternal goodness of God, who would not permit such injustices to stand unchallenged. And David invited the hearers of this maskil to join him in putting their trust in the Lord whose righteousness rules the universe.

Such assurances are sometimes difficult to credit. If God punishes evil and rewards goodness (as we also believe), it is not necessarily a transaction that fits into our narrow attention span. God does not settle all accounts by Saturday evening. Often we must wait on the Lord, and when the waiting stretches beyond the limits of our comfort, we have only one elixir to soothe our anxiety: trust. Though it often seems little comfort in the interminable stretch between promise and reward, it is our trust in God that keeps us on course.

DAY 53
Read Psalm 53

A careful reader of the psalms will note that this psalm is almost an exact duplicate of Psalm 14. The differences are editorial rather than substantive. What can account for this inclusion of two psalms that are so similar to each other?

We must remember that the written word was very rarely seen at the time the psalms were written. Many people lived their entire lives without ever seeing a printed edition of any scripture. The psalms were intended to be heard, learned through repetition, and sung or spoken from memory. It would not be surprising if in their verbal transfer from generation to generation, a few variations in the text might occur. The surprising thing is not that the versions in Psalms 14 and 53 are slightly different, but that they are so similar.

When the Dead Sea Scrolls were discovered at Qumran in 1948, Bible scholars rejoiced to learn that there were many manuscripts, dating from 100 B.C.E. to 100 C.E., that were the earliest versions of several of the Old Testament books—centuries earlier than any previously discovered manuscripts. Great care was exercised in preserving the scrolls and translating them. When the translations were complete, the scholars carefully compared them with the versions of those books we have in our Bibles, and they discovered that the differences were minor and superficial, requiring no changes in our understanding of those books!

The fact is that God's word is ineradicably true, immovably secure, firmly grounded, and eternally reliable. And the God whose word it is will defend the holy truth against evil challenges and human weaknesses. Truly it is a fool who says in his or her heart that there is no God. And equally foolish is the one who questions whether the word of God is true.

Like the essence of these two psalms, the authentic teaching of God is "the same yesterday and today and forever" (Hebrews 13:8).

A woman who had grown up reading the *King James Version* of the Bible complained when she read a selection in a newer version: "They keep changing the word of God." But no one can do that. We can (and should) change the language to make the truth understandable to new generations, but the truth of God cannot be changed.

A Texas sportswriter once swore he could stand on the sidelines, shut his eyes, and identify tackles made by E. J. Holub, an All-America linebacker at Texas Tech and later a professional standout. "When Holub hits somebody, it has a distinctive sound," said the writer. "It sounds like a crate of curtain rods falling three stories and landing flat on the sidewalk."

Did you ever wonder what sound the Christian message has? Many think it has the sound of a wet dishrag flapping in the wind, that the Christian faith is an escape from life. It is sentimentality, group weakness, dependence. The church is for kids, old people, and women. No red-blooded, adventuresome, responsible, mature person would be caught dead in the church!

But a quick reading of the psalms of David gives us a distinctly different view of faith and piety. David did not ask of God a warm and safe closet in which to hide, but a Presence on the battlefield that would keep him going when the fighting was the most fierce and the enemies the most ingenious. He requested no immunity from trouble, but strength in the midst of it.

An old Persian legend tells of a king who asked his wise men to prepare a comprehensive history of humankind so that he might learn to rule wisely. He gave them twenty years for the task. They finally brought him 10,000 volumes. The king sent them back to cut it down. Ten years later they returned with 5,000 volumes. "I don't have time to read all that," he said. "Go back and compress your work into a smaller space." Again and again they came to the king with volumes for him to read. Finally the king cried, "Time is failing. My eyesight is going. Compress what you have written into the smallest possible space." At the end of a year the chief wise man came and said, "Here it is, your majesty. We have wrapped up the history of humankind into a single sentence. It is this: They were born; they suffered; and they died."

At times for all of us—and all the time for some of us—life is a battlefield, and the service of our faith is not to remove us from the scene of battle, but to strengthen us, refresh us, and give us the assurance of victory.

DAY 55

As we noted in yesterday's reflection, the facing of burdens is an inescapable lot of all humankind. But not all burdens are to be dealt with in the same manner. The Bible suggests three ways of dealing with our burdens. At first glance, the ways seem to be contradictory, but taken together they provide the complete answer we are all looking for. The first of these three elements in the prescription is in Galatians 6:5: "For all must carry their own loads." The soul is like a muscle that does not gain strength until it strains to do something that is difficult. An experienced mountaineer accompanied a young mountain climber on a difficult ascent. At one point the climb was particularly arduous and dangerous, and the path was rough with jagged stones. The young climber complained, "I wish there weren't so many bumps in the path." The experienced climber said, "The bumps are what you climb on."

Christian discipleship is a difficult road, and to have reached the heights you have already attained is proof that you have had some high hills to climb. But all the easy roads lead down.

Equally important is the second element in the prescription for dealing with our burdens. It is again from the sixth chapter of Galatians: "Bear one another's burdens, and in this way you will fulfill the law of Christ" (Galatians 6:2). Every one of us has had experiences in which the grace of God was conveyed to us through the simple ministries of a Christian friend who knew us and knew God and had just the right words to link our need with God's help.

Finally, like a pleasant oasis in the midst of a desert, there is a verse in Psalm 55 that provides the energizing principle for successful dealings with our burdens: "Cast your burden on the LORD, and he will sustain you" (v. 22). Note that it does not say that if we cast our burdens on the Lord, the Lord will remove the burdens. Often God does not do that. But God can—and does—sustain us so that we find ourselves able to bear burdens courageously and triumphantly.

A department-store customer saw a woman getting on the elevator struggling to carry several large and heavy parcels. As the elevator started its journey several floors to the top, the observer suggested, "Why don't you put your burdens down? The elevator will carry them up for you." Even when we think we are carrying our burdens by ourselves, there is a power that is carrying both us and our burdens. "I made you," the Lord says, "I know you, and I will carry you." And you will be sustained.

DAY 56
Read Psalm 56

Many people have a "foxhole approach" to religion. They believe that the Christian faith is most meaningful–or only meaningful–when disaster threatens and all other comforts fail us. When skies are blue and the stock market is attaining new heights, we don't need God, thank you. We can very well take care of ourselves. But let the threat of pain or poverty or death raise its ugly head, and we all beat it to the foxhole and raise the white flag of piety.

Where did we get the idea that God is an escape hatch from the real world? It seems that God has a lousy reputation for getting people off the hook. The fact is, God's forte seems to be getting people *on* the hook.

To be sure, faith in God is relevant and helpful in every situation, death included. But the question of faith is the same whether you find yourself cheering on your favorite basketball team or pacing the corridors of a hospital emergency room awaiting words that will forever change your life.

Faith is not a resignation from the human lot or a pitiful plea for some undeserved withdrawal from earthly responsibility. It is the most realistic, the most practical, and the most hopeful life stance one can take: recognizing the most powerful force in the universe and tapping that power in the fulfillment of assigned duties now, in this moment, and here, in this square foot of earth where we stand. Unless we are like the fools who say there is no God, we must surely realize that plotting a life without taking into consideration the Lord of this manor, who owns both us and the earth where we live, is more than just the height of nincompoopery. It is sinfully stupid.

A charming phrase in this psalm says, "Put my tears in your bottle" (v. 8). Royal personages in those days believed that their tears were especially precious, so they kept the evidence of their weeping in a small vial. When David asked God to put his own tears in God's bottle, he was asking God to share his feelings of grief, sorrow, and fear. And that is exactly what God did on Calvary. Such a God may be trusted, not only when we are in the foxhole of trouble, but when we are dancing in the gazebo of joy.

DAY 57
Read Psalm 57

Once again the heading of this psalm gives a strange but meaningful instruction, which clarifies the thought in the song that follows: "To the leader: Do Not Destroy." It is possible that the reference here is to a tune to be used in singing the psalm. "Do Not Destroy" might seem a strange name for a tune, but what follows in this ancient writing is a series of truths that are too important to forget. Perhaps we would name it, "Changeless Truth in a Changing World," or "Thoughts Too True to Be Discarded."

Here we read the contrast between the eternally dependable and the storms of destruction that "pass by." Wise, indeed, is that person who can distinguish between the merely urgent and the definitely important.

Like all the rest of us, David could avoid the vicissitudes and perils of life in this world. But he drew confidence and strength from the things that survived long after the storms had passed.

He begins with a familiar picture: a mother hen gathering her chicks under her protective wings. To a chick there is no shelter more cherished than its mother's protective love.

A Christian woman who trusted in the assurance of this psalm got into her automobile one night to drive home after a meeting at the church. Not until after she had started her car did she realize that a man with evil intent had hidden in the back seat behind her. When he began to make his threatening moves, the woman began to say something over and over that the intruder did not understand, but which he feared. He quickly opened the door of the car and escaped, complaining, "That lady is crazy. She kept yelling, 'I'm covered with feathers! I'm covered with feathers!'" She was recalling, in her own words, the assurance of this psalm: "In the shadow of your wings I will take refuge" (v. 1).

Everyone may have his or her own understanding of how this truth works out in practical application. But if our trust is in God, we can all claim triumphantly, "I am covered with feathers!"

DAY 58

Psalm 58 is not an easy psalm to read, especially for Christian people, who have heard the word of Jesus, "Love your enemies and pray for those who persecute you" (Matthew 5:44). Perhaps it is easier to accept this writing when we view it as a period piece, accurately reflecting the thinking of the time in which it was composed. It was a black-and-white world the psalmist lived in. Only the righteous deserved the blessing of God, and nothing but destruction awaited the evil.

But the real world in which we live is one in which good and evil cannot be found in an unmixed state. As an old verse says:

> There is so much good in the worst of us,
> and so much bad in the best of us,
> that it hardly behooves any of us
> to talk about the rest of us.

Given our human weaknesses and tendencies, we must concede that all of us live in glass houses that discourage our own stone throwing.

In a classic Peanuts strip, Charlie Brown, in a philosophical mood, asks, "Why are some people good and some people bad? And who decides who is good and who is bad?" Lucy eagerly responds, "I will!" Many people are only too ready to make that determination. But Jesus' admonition, "Do not judge, so that you may not be judged" (Matthew 7:1), warns us against usurping the authority of God, who reserves that prerogative for the court of heaven.

Nevertheless, the basic rule built into the universe is that whatever is good will survive and be strengthened, and whatever is evil will be destroyed and eventually disappear.

Each of us, by our own attitudes and actions, contributes to the sum total of good or evil in the world. God is the unrelenting foe of all that is wrong and the dependable protector and preserver of all that is right. And each of us chooses which side we'll be on.

Back in the not-so-good-old days when some avant-garde theologians were shaking up the pious establishment by declaring, as Friedrich Wilhelm Nietzsche had, that "God is dead," one enterprising pastor caught a ride on the publicity bandwagon by declaring, "God is not dead; He's only asleep." To substantiate his bizarre claim, he cited various pervasive evils in our society that no self-respecting God would permit if awake. The drug culture, the sexual revolution, violence in the cities, and certain other blemishes on the face of our culture were cited as Exhibits A through Z to prove that God–if still in the business of being God–had at least nodded off.

Similarly, in this psalm David assumes that the only plausible explanation for God's apparent apathy in the face of evil is that God has fallen asleep at the switch. And David skates perilously close to heresy when he demands of God, "Rouse yourself, come to my help...Awake to punish all the nations" (vv. 4, 5).

When Elijah had the historic contest with the priests of Baal in the heights of Mount Carmel, the prophet taunted the impotent Baal worshipers by suggesting to them that their god was inactive because he was asleep. "Cry aloud," Elijah mocked them. "Surely he is a god; either he is meditating, or he has wandered away, or he is on a journey, or perhaps he is asleep and must be awakened" (1 Kings 18:27). But one cannot awaken a lifeless idol.

But our "God is not dead, nor doth he sleep," as Longfellow reminded us. And another psalm asserts, "He who keeps you will not slumber. He who keeps Israel will neither slumber nor sleep" (Psalm 121:3–4).

Perhaps we should ask ourselves, when evil triumphs in this world, who is it that is really asleep?

Rabindranath Tagore, an Indian mystic, was once so appalled by the suffering children on the crowded streets of Calcutta that he lifted his tear-filled eyes to heaven in the reproach, "God, why don't you do something about all this?" And he reported that the answer came to him from heaven: "I most certainly have done something about it. I made you."

If evil thrives where you live, who is it that is really asleep?

DAY 60
Read Psalm 60

Many a Christian hymn has been cruelly truncated by the modern inclination to keep everything in a worship service "short and snappy." We shy away from such Christmas carols as "While Shepherds Watched Their Flocks by Night" because Nahum Tate was so undisciplined as to allow his lyrics to run on to an outrageous six stanzas. It would possibly have been dropped from the repertoire of the church entirely except for the instant pruning effected by many a careless pastor who announces, "Let us now sing hymn number 573, the first, second, and last stanzas, standing on the last." But the meat of many a hymn may be found in that part of it that is frequently omitted in the effort to get everyone out in time to beat the Baptists at the nearby cafeteria for Sunday dinner.

A study of these neglected lyrics provides the information that Martin Luther's immortal "A Mighty Fortress Is Our God" comprised a full thirteen verses. Although what is left in the four stanzas usually printed in our hymnals provides enough grist to feed all the theological mills we are capable of operating, the abandoned words add clarity to the theme of the hymn. Especially significant is the last stanza, which Luther intended to be the ringing commission that would set the Christians' feet to marching as they departed from the worship service to face, again, the rigors and perils of the world.

The last half of that intended last stanza says:

Were they to take our house,
goods, honor, child, or spouse;
though life be wrenched away,
they cannot win the day.
The Kingdom's ours forever!

Such was Luther's confidence as he faced excommunication, persecution, and the defection of former friends. And such was the psalmist's resolution as he viewed the losses and dangers of past, present, and future. This much, at least, was true: The kingdom of God was his forever.

And that kingdom is ours forever.

Isn't that enough to go on?

DAY 61
Read Psalm 61

One of the more threadbare movie devices is the dramatic (melodramatic?) scene in which a man declares his undying love for his sweetheart by saying, "This is something that is bigger than the both of us!" Of course, in his next movie he will be equally passionate about some other actress. But all of us long to find something to cling to that is bigger than we are and has resources beyond our own.

So the psalmist says, "Lead me to the rock that is higher than I" (v. 2). Israel is a rugged land, with torturous deserts and jagged mountains. Violent storms arise quickly, endangering the lives of hapless travelers. Even the sparse trees offer scant security. The only real security in the time of storm may be found in the giant rocks, which often have caves or fissures of a size to provide shelter for one or more human beings.

It was probably that picture that the psalmist intended us to derive from the plea: "Lead me to the rock that is higher than I." A smaller rock would be a useless shelter, but one that is "bigger than the both of us" could be trusted to provide the security needed in a time of storm.

Several Christian hymns have borrowed this idiom. "Rock of Ages, cleft for me, let me hide myself in thee," says one such hymn. And another declares, "On Christ the solid rock I stand, all other ground is sinking sand."

One of the most tragic realities of human life is that so many people have given their lives in pursuit of things that are smaller than they are. Like Esau, they surrender their birthright for a mess of pottage or some other prize that has fleeting worth.

Benjamin Franklin related that he learned his first lesson in thrift when, as a small boy, he saw in a store window a whistle that he wanted to own. He emptied his piggy bank and surrendered all the coins in it to the astonished merchant, who nevertheless took his childish treasure in exchange for the whistle.

You have only so many hours to live, so much strength to expend, so much loyalty you can give. Be sure that what you buy with your currencies of time, strength, and ability is something that is bigger than you.

DAY 62
Read Psalm 62

Twice in this psalm the theme is pronounced, "For God alone my soul waits in silence" (vv. 1, 5). The word *waits,* as used in the Bible, has a distinctly different meaning than the one we ordinarily attach to that short word. We think of waiting as an inactive marking of time. "Staying or remaining in expectation of an anticipated event," the dictionary says. It carries the sense of lingering or delaying. And that expresses the attitude many people have about God. "Why doesn't God do something about the evil in the world?" we ask. But it is a moot question. We have no great interest in the answer or its implications. Like Jonah sitting under the shadow of his gourd vine, waiting for God to punish the wicked citizens of Nineveh, we are content to sit and watch while God does God's thing.

But there is another meaning of the word *wait,* and here it is: To wait is to perform the duties of a waiter in a restaurant, to determine the wishes of the diners, and to make them comfortable and provide for their needs. When we "wait on God," that doesn't mean we sit idly by, watching for God to burst into action and do something Godlike. It means that we present ourselves to God—as a waiter does to a diner in a restaurant—to determine what God wants of us, and then we do everything we can to please God and to fulfill God's wishes.

So the phrase "For God alone my soul waits in silence" implies that the psalmist is at God's disposal, willing to be an instrument in God's hands.

Have you ever gone to a restaurant and sat at a table hungry and knowing exactly what you would like to eat, but the waiter, busy with other chores, ignores you?

Maybe that's how God feels when there is so much to be done, and God knows what needs to be done but lacks the willing hands to apply themselves to the task. We are accustomed to praying to God, beseeching God to get busy and finish the work of creation. Perhaps we have reproached God, demanding, "God, why don't you do something about the state of the world?" What if God were suddenly to rend the heavens with the question to us: "Why don't *you* do something about this?" If you wait on God—really *wait on God*—God's wish will be your command.

DAY 63
Read Psalm 63

Traveling south from Jericho to the Dead Sea, in "the wilderness of Judea," one sees a highway sign identifying that lonely and desolate spot as "the lowest point on earth." More than 1,300 feet below sea level and having only about two inches of rainfall a year, it is indeed a desolate and forbidding place. The highest temperature ever recorded (129 degrees Fahrenheit) occurred there on June 21, 1942. Biblical scholars believe that it was in that area that Jesus withstood his grueling forty days of temptation.

It was to this "wilderness of Judea" that David fled to escape the murderous wrath of his former friend, King Saul. Little wonder Saul did not pursue David there: Saul was nothing if not practical! But it was while David was a fugitive in that forsaken place that he wrote this psalm (or at least formulated it in his mind, to be transcribed later).

Lonely, frightened, angry, and wondering perhaps if even God had abandoned him, David found the ambience of the area a perfect match for his spirits. Picture him languishing for food, parched from the lack of water, crying out his lament to God, "My soul thirsts for you; my flesh faints for you, as in a dry and weary land where there is no water" (v. 1).

Who of us has not suffered the anguish and agony of "the wilderness of Judea?" Jacob found his "wilderness of Judea" at the ford of the Jabbok, where his sins caught up with him and forced him to recognize that God could be the enemy. The whole nation of Israel struggled through their "wilderness of Judea" experience through forty years of privation and sacrifice. Elijah suffered his "wilderness of Judea" experience when Jezebel put out a contract on his life and his despair left him feeling that even God had deserted him.

But no matter how forbidding the place or circumstance of our torment, we need to remember that however forsaken we may feel, there is no experience in human life that will leave us *God*-forsaken. It was in recognition of that fact that David was able to rejoice, "Your steadfast love is better than life" (v. 3).

Following his historic duel with the devil in his wilderness experience, Jesus found that in that torturous place, "angels came and waited on him" (Matthew 4:11).

Whatever evils populate your "wilderness of Judea," God's angels are there too!

We are fond of recalling that old schoolyard taunt, "Sticks and stones may break my bones, but words can never hurt me." But for all the meager comfort that saying may provide for the one who seeks to use it in self-defense, it is simply not true. Words have greater power to injure us than any physical violence can inflict. Words have an astonishing power either to hurt or to heal. That's why Jesus spoke in such stern terms when he warned us, "I tell you, on the day of judgment you will have to give an account for every careless word you utter; for by your words you will be justified, and by your words you will be condemned" (Matthew 12:36–37).

If that means that when we are called to the great judgment seat, we will have to listen to a recording of everything we ever said and give an accounting for it in the white light of eternal clarity, it would be difficult to think of any greater punishment!

The psalmist had obviously suffered from the words spoken by his enemies. Exactly what those words were, or what they meant to accomplish, or how they affected the psalmist can only be guessed at. What is clear is that there were those who meant to do harm to the psalmist and who devised some cruel plot to achieve the psalmist's downfall. They schemed and whispered and devised some ambush to trap the psalmist. But whether the psalmist ever stepped into that snare was beside the point: The real damage was done by the words.

Are there those who have been given pain because of words you have spoken—words of anger, a false report, a morsel of gossip, a thoughtless remark that belittled or judged? One can no more unsay a word than one can unring a bell. Words take on a life of their own and may continue to cause pain long after we have forgotten that we said them.

Before saying anything, we might well ask ourselves, "Is it true? Is it fair? Will anyone be hurt by it? Will it be better left unsaid? Would I be glad I spoke these words if, on the day of judgment, our Lord plays those words back to me?"

DAY 65
Read Psalm 65

In this lyrical psalm that celebrates the beauty and bounty of the earth, there is a surprising statement that reaches out, in a seemingly irrelevant tangent, to one of the most mature theological assumptions in the Old Testament: "To you all flesh shall come" (v. 2). Such a statement rattles the rafters of our reverence and reverberates throughout our systematic theology and sends shock waves through our narrow view of what constitutes the community of God's people.

"All flesh"–that means all people, every last person on this earth: the good and the bad, the orthodox and the renegade, the conservative and the liberal, the theologically correct and those who wouldn't recognize a theological statement if they met one head-on in the middle of the Sahara Desert. "All flesh" includes not just all Christians, or all monotheists, or all believers, or all decent human beings, but "all flesh."

And what is it that is said of that gigantic mob of people who are included in that phrase? It says that they will all come to God. Not *may come,* though even that thought would have been angrily rejected as heresy in years past in many quarters. And even today such a presumption would be dismissed as the empty-headed claim of someone whose theology is a mile wide and an inch deep. "All flesh" shall come to God.

Surely that means that God does not, by a snap of holy fingers, decide the eternal fate of anyone or gleefully jerk the rug out from under those whose petition for entrance into the kingdom of heaven came too late or in the wrong grammar or logic. Although it strains our ability to comprehend such generosity, we must come to terms with the fact that as much as God cares about you–and that's more than you can possibly imagine–God cares at least that much (and maybe more) for those who claim to be atheists, or who live like them. And long after your paltry patience has been exhausted by their blind stupidity, God will still be loving them, inviting them, and drawing them–kicking and screaming all the way–into God's loving arms.

And if some people do, indeed, succeed in going to hell, it will have to be accomplished over the objection of the fierce, never-surrendering love of God.

And if God loves "all flesh" to that extent, surely we must find a way to love them too.

DAY 66
Read Psalm 66

"Listen, my children, and you shall hear
Of the midnight ride of Paul Revere."

So begins Longfellow's famous poem, in which one of America's cherished legends is reported and conveyed to the next generation. It was in the same spirit that the psalmist said in this psalm, "Come and hear, all you who fear God, and I will tell what he has done for me" (v. 16). It was in this spirit that all scripture was written and published. To preserve and perpetuate the earliest legends of life on this created planet the five books of the Pentateuch were finally transferred from the spoken word to a written document. Those five books—Genesis, Exodus, Leviticus, Numbers, and Deuteronomy—are all an effort by people who, under the name of Moses, wanted to pass on the record of God's activity in the world.

Each of the gospels—Matthew, Mark, Luke, and John—is a written record of someone's personal experience with the Christ. "Here is what happened to me," was their testimony.

And each of us has an obligation to find some way to share our witness, to tell the story as we have experienced it, to those who have not heard. And if the Christian faith is to survive beyond the present generation, we must make sure that the children have heard our stories. To be sure, we do not have at our disposal the perverse resources that are being spent by the forces of unrighteousness to seduce the minds of our young. But we do have one advantage that cannot be matched: We have the simple but powerful window into the soul of a child that has always been the most effective means of education—the power of a positive, personal influence and a clear and honest witness of how the Christian faith has done its magnificent work in our own lives.

Not even Billy Graham or Pope John Paul II has the kind of influence you have over your own children or the children that have been drawn into your life network by your love and concern for them. And you need no one else's story to tell or any other lesson to convey. Just tell them who you are, and what you are, because of Christ in your life. That's the story the world needs to hear.

DAY 67

The father of several small children was sitting in his easy chair reading the newspaper at the end of a busy day. Presently one of his daughters peeked around the newspaper and asked if he could take time to explain an arithmetic problem she had brought home from school. He patiently laid the paper aside and showed her how to work the problem.

Next came a young son who had fallen down in his play in the yard. Tears streamed down his cheeks and he wailed loudly for attention. "Fix it, Daddy!" was the request. And with kisses appropriately placed at the site of the hurt and caressing words, the father administered the healing that parents know how to provide.

Finally the youngest—a three-year-old girl—poked his knee with her tiny finger as a signal that more attention was called for. "And what do you want?" the father asked, in mock severity. With an ingenuous smile she replied, "I just want to sit in your lap."

And so she did, with blessings given and received by both.

So after many psalms of complaint and demand, we come to one of those beautiful expressions of trust and gratitude that make the heart sing. It is a psalm that is more appropriately sung than spoken. No bitter resentments spill out here, and no demands on God, just a simple and grateful expression of love for God. If only we always knew how much God deserves our thankful praise and how much God surely delights in such expressions! How richer our own lives would be if we lived every day in parentheses of thanks. How much more easily our burdens could be borne, how much more patiently our problems could be solved if we knew that God is as ready and willing to attend to our needs as is a loving parent.

A little girl was sleeping alone in her new bedroom for the first time. She was a bit frightened by the strange shadows she saw and the unfamiliar noises in her new surroundings. To reassure herself, she called to her father, who was in the next room.

"Daddy," she called, "are you here?" "Yes, Christy, Daddy is here," was the comforting reply. "Daddy, are you awake?" "Yes, Christy, Daddy is awake."

After a few moments of silence one last question came: "And Daddy, is your face turned toward me?"

So the psalmist said, "May God be gracious to us and bless us and make his face to shine upon us" (v. 1). God's face is turned toward us.

DAY 68
Read Psalm 68

The sixty-eighth psalm, despite the resonance and beauty of many of its phrases, is a most difficult writing to understand. Many scholars have agreed that this is the most stubbornly obscure of all the psalms. It is not a writing that can be reduced to a concise outline, but rather, seems to be a rummage sale of leftovers and miscellaneous tidbits of information and inspiration. The way to enjoy this psalm is not to see it as a whole, as we do many of the others, but to pick up the gems one at a time and let the light shine on and through them.

One such morsel, contained in a few words unrelated to the rest of the psalm, is the information that God has a special concern for people of special needs. "Father of orphans and protector of widows is God in his holy habitation. God gives the desolate a home to live in; he leads out the prisoners to prosperity" (vv. 5–6).

At first glance these words give us comfort. But on deeper reflection we begin to realize that most of us do not fall into those categories. We are not widows (most of us) or orphans (at least early in our lives). We are certainly not desolate, for we are surrounded by family and friends, a community of God's people in which we are cherished, and a God who has never abandoned us. And we are not prisoners. Is it possible that God cares about all these people with special needs *more* than God cares about us?

It is a most consoling thought to realize that God loves *us*. We easily accept that thought, almost as if it is our right to claim such divine affection. But sometimes it comes as a great shock to us to realize that God loves other people too, every bit as much as God loves us. And it makes us distinctly uncomfortable to learn that God even loves those people whom we don't love at all!

In a former generation it was common for the Christian in the group to remind others, when some absent person was being maligned, that the person being talked about was "one for whom Christ died."

Shouldn't it soften and refine all our attitudes toward other people to be reminded that God loves them? And what does it do to our relationship with God if we hate or hurt someone God loves that much?

DAY 69
Read Psalm 69

Born in many of us is an instinctive fear of water. We have many idiomatic phrases that reflect this fear. "In deep water," we say, to identify an unmanageable circumstance that has engulfed us. "Up the creek without a paddle" is our way of describing a situation over which we have no control. "In over our heads" conveys a problem with which most of us are familiar. And when we are exerting great effort but making no progress, we describe our fruitless activity as "treading water."

So the psalmist describes dangers and discomforts by using this common idiom: "The waters have come up to my neck...I have come into deep waters, and the flood sweeps over me" (vv. 1–2).

But a jarring contradiction is suggested in the next verse: "I am weary with my crying; my throat is parched." The throat is parched? At the very moment when the psalmist is so inundated by water comes a complaint of being thirsty!

Ernest Campbell, former pastor of Riverside Church in New York City, titled one of his books *Locked in a Room with Open Doors*. The title was derived from a strange phobia on the part of his younger brother, who had an irrational fear of open doors. To taunt him, his older brother would threaten to lock him up in a room with open doors.

What a metaphor to describe people who are paralyzed in the face of great opportunities and liberties.

So the psalmist was dying of thirst while the water was lapping at his nose. Can that be an accurate picture of ourselves, sometimes, when we suffer for the lack of resources that are plenteously abundant all around us?

"Lonely in a crowd" is another expression of this. All around us are people whose hearts and minds are open to us and who need friends as much as we do. But some isolationist fear of others keeps us from opening our hearts to them. Do we long for significance and meaning in our lives? We are surrounded, on every side, by opportunities for contributions that would make our lives worthwhile.

When you're in deep water, you have two choices: You can be drowned or baptized. The choice is yours.

A harried mother of several small children is reported to have demanded of God, "Lord, give me patience! *And I want it right now!*" Such is the urgent plea of the psalmist in this brief document. Its very brevity suggests that there is no time for flowery eloquence or theological correctness. (This is the shortest of the psalms thus far in the collection. It is not the most brief, however, for Psalm 117 contains but two verses.)

Here is a prayer on the run, an out-of-breath request for rescue. What exactly the writer was running from we can only guess, but there is no doubt of the urgency of the plea. This being so, it can serve well as a generic prayer suitable for a multitude of crises that confront us with fierce and unrelenting determination.

In an old recitation that was well known to our grandparents, a preacher is taking a walk through the woods when an angry bear suddenly confronts him. In his hasty retreat the preacher demands of God, "Lord, if you can't help me, at least don't help that bear!"

And there is some hint, in this psalm, of the writer's grudging reminder to God that he is, after all, on the Lord's side, and the Lord ought, therefore, to help him and not his enemies. The righteous deserve to prosper, don't they? Those who are on God's side should realize some benefit from that allegiance, shouldn't they? Instead, those persistent enemies cackle "Aha! Aha!" over the misfortunes of the godly.

What the psalmist is asking of God, therefore, is to wake up and tend to business.

"Let all who seek you rejoice and be glad" (v. 4). There ought to be some tangible, recognizable benefits to seeking God. "Let those who love your salvation say evermore, 'God is great!'" (v. 4).

But often the rewards of a godly life can't be reduced to the small change of instant proofs that fit into the cash register drawer of our understandings. Indeed, it is when we can't see the results of our faith that our belief in God is really faith, and not some superficial counterfeit of it.

But even when we don't realize it, God is listening to our prayers and preparing the right answer. And the benefit of our faith is not that God is actively, lovingly present in our troubles, but that we know that and depend on it.

DAY 71
Read Psalm 71

A pastor was making one of her frequent calls on the oldest member of her flock, an elderly man who had passed his hundredth birthday. The pastor found it difficult to remain cheerful and optimistic when calling on the old man, because a miscellany of the man's pains and problems had robbed him of his good nature. On that particular day, he was especially critical and full of complaints. Finally he asked, "Pastor, why doesn't the Lord call me home? My wife and children are all gone, and my friends have gone ahead of me. Why doesn't the Lord call me home?"

Seeking to be helpful, the pastor replied, "Maybe the Lord has something for you to do." "Well," came the grumpy response, "I ain't a-gonna do it!"

Despite the sentimentality that frequently pictures "the golden years" as a time of rest and the reaping of rewards, there is truth in the saying, "Old Age Is Not for Sissies."

To be sure, there are perils and problems lying in wait for the youth. But every age presents its unique challenges.

The writer of Psalm 71 was obviously a person who had achieved a mature age. "Do not cast me off in the time of old age," (v. 9). "So even to old age and gray hairs, O God, do not forsake me" (v. 18). Perhaps the greater danger is not that God might forsake us, but that we might forsake God. No longer does the elderly person face the temptations of passion and ambition. But there are snares nonetheless. It is so easy when one is full of years to become cynical and critical, to stop hoping, to stop believing that partnership with God is possible.

But the psalmist refuses to fall into those snares. "I will hope continually, and will praise you yet more and more" (v. 14). The same attitude lit up the last chapter of the apostle Paul's life. As a man of years he said, "I do not consider that I have made it my own: but this one thing I do: forgetting what lies behind and straining forward to what lies ahead, I press on" (Philippians 3:13–14). Then to those of us who are full of years, Paul adds this challenge: "Let those of us then who are mature be of the same mind" (Philippians 3:15).

Even on the last day of life, our direction should still be heavenward.

Here is one of the most beautiful writings in the whole collection of psalms. There is not a word of complaint or lament, only an encomium and a proffered cornucopia of blessings for the leader of the land. Since the heading identifies this psalm as directed "Of Solomon," we may conclude that it was written on the occasion of Solomon's coronation, perhaps to be read as a part of the ceremony. Certainly the rich imagery and picturesque wording hint that this may have been a major effort on the part of the "poet laureate" of Israel, if such a position existed.

Let these words wash over your listening heart:

> May he live while the sun endures,
>   and as long as the moon, throughout all generations.
> May he be like rain that falls on the mown grass,
>   like showers that water the earth.
> In his days may righteousness flourish
>   and peace abound, until the moon is no more. (vv. 5–7)

What a blessing to be given such a tribute, and what a challenge to fulfill its promise!

Unfortunately, Solomon did not fulfill the claims of that graceful platform. But the attributes suggested would be worthy aims for anyone. Especially noteworthy is the sentence "May he be like rain that falls on the mown grass." Can you think of a more pleasant picture, a more picturesque description of the freshness and prosperity and peace that God wants all people to possess?

Twice in this psalm the Hebrew word *shalom* is found. In the first instance (v. 3) it is translated "prosperity." In the seventh verse it is given the usual translation of "peace." But the word clearly means more than an absence of war. It means the presence of freshness and the joy of spiritual prosperity. It implies a society in which everyone's contribution is valued and everyone's need is honored. Blessed, indeed, is the person whose very presence creates an atmosphere of *shalom*. And everyone can make that kind of difference.

But we all know that there are some people who bring happiness wherever they go, and others who bring happiness *whenever* they go. And in this world there are not enough people in the first classification!

"Amen and Amen" (v. 19). With this double "Lord, make it so," Book II of Psalms ends.

DAY 73
Read Psalm 73

As a corollary to the theme pronounced in previous psalms (Why do bad things happen to good people?), this psalm asks, "Why do good things happen to bad people?" It is a theme found in many places in the Bible, especially the book of Job, which demands of God, "Why do the wicked prosper?" It is a puzzle to many who have been faithful in their obedience to God and yet have not received the rewards seemingly reaped by those who cannot claim such spiritual credentials. "Why do the wicked live on, reach old age, and grow mighty in power?" (Job 21:7).

A cartoon pictured a small boy kneeling beside his bed for his nighttime prayer. But his prayer became a complaint: "Mama is still irritable; Tommy didn't pass his arithmetic test; and Daddy's hair is still falling out. I'm tired of saying the prayers for this family and not getting any results!" And it is a problem for people who earnestly pray for the right things to happen to people they care about. But they observe other families in which the mothers are not irritable, the brothers comfortably pass their arithmetic exams, and their fathers keep a full head of hair even though they have no devout little boy praying for them. How can God allow such injustices to befall those who are, after all, on God's side? It is enough to shake one's faith!

And so the psalmist fell victim to a fading of his faith, not because his prayers went unanswered, but because those who didn't pray seemed to be getting along very well. Many of us have found ourselves in that same sad predicament, how to keep our faith when the good continue to suffer and the bad persistently prosper. To seek a solution, the psalmist did something that always helps when our faith flickers. He went to church. "I went into the sanctuary of God; then I perceived their end" (v. 17). It was in his worship experience that he realized the truth that while God does not reward every good deed and punish every evil act with instantaneous, mathematical precision, God has put into good and evil the seeds of ultimate justice. Whatever the current scene may insinuate, God's governance of the universe will ultimately honor the right and those who have upheld it.

Or, as a more recent observer has suggested, "When the outlook is dark, try the uplook."

DAY 74
Read Psalm 74

It was a morning of mourning, never to be forgotten, in the city of Milan, Italy.

During the previous night, World War II bombers had dropped their devastating cargo on the city, reducing instantly to rubble many of the historic buildings in Milan, including the beautiful little church of Santa Maria delle Grazie. It was an ancient building, constructed in the latter years of the fifteenth century.

The church had been built as evidence of the Christian faith espoused by the populace. But the church was best known for the painting that decorated one wall of the lower level. It was *The Last Supper,* created by Leonardo da Vinci. In the years that followed its creation, Leonardo's masterpiece was subjected to numerous acts of vandalism and neglect. The little church had been pressed into service as a barracks for Napoleon's troops in 1797, with the painted wall sheltering the horses of the troops billeted there. At other points in its history that wall had been covered with the kitchen grease of the refectory that fed the monks of the monastery located in the building. At one time a door was clumsily chopped through the painting to ease the serving of the meals.

Perhaps even more cruel were the crude attempts to restore the painting to its original beauty with a free-flowing paintbrush. But no barbarity would equal the devastation of the bombs of World War II.

That morning, after the attack, pious members of the parish began to remove—carefully, reverently—the pieces of rubble that covered the wall. And they discovered, to their astonishment, that the rubble that covered the wall also protected it from permanent damage. And when all the debris had been cleared away, they found Leonardo's great masterpiece completely intact. It was almost as if to demonstrate that there are some landmarks so sacred, so faithful, and so important that the ravages of time cannot erase them.

Such was the discovery of the people of God when, in this psalm, they lamented the destruction of the temple. All its holy emblems had been destroyed. "We do not see our emblems," the people sighed (v. 9), as they recalled that the temple had served as a signboard to God and God's truth.

But of far greater importance than the signs that point to God—signs that may be destroyed—is the fact that God is present, even when there seem to be no signs pointing to God. The day and the night, the summer and the winter, and the stars and the sun all point to the hand of a God who cannot be destroyed.

DAY 75
Read Psalm 75

It is an old story, worn thin from much use at political rallies to illustrate the dark sin of party disloyalty. A voter who had always given his support to a certain perennial candidate had given notice of his intention, at the forthcoming election, to support the incumbent's opponent. The incumbent heard of this threatened defection and at a political rally called his former supporter aside and confronted him. "How can you do this to me?" the politician asked. "After all I have done for you! Don't you remember when I got you the job you still have? And have you forgotten that I managed to get the street in front of your house repaired? And I was the one who got a scholarship for your son. And if you've forgotten all that, how can you forget the time I gave a blood transfusion to save your life?" "Oh, I remember all that," the defector said with a wave of the hand. "But what have you done for me lately?"

How sad it is that we have such a short memory concerning our blessings, but such an endless recollection of grudges! And few of us express any gratitude to God for blessings granted us in the past, though they may have greatly enriched our lives at the time. Yesterday's good health is all but forgotten when present ailments and troubles befall us.

A bit of verse celebrates the length of a dachshund—"a sausage hound."

> There was a dachshund once so long it hadn't any notion
> how long it took to notify his tail of his emotion.
> And so it happened when his eyes were filled with tears of sadness,
> his little tail kept wagging on because of previous gladness.

Real thanksgiving to God is not based on a ledger-sheet balance of current assets, but a joyous recognition that God has been with us all along the days, both in the sunshine and in the storms.

When we give our grateful praise to God, we are celebrating not what we have, but what God is. And what God is, is faithful—every day, in every circumstance, forever.

DAY 76
Read Psalm 76

The previous psalm asserts, "People tell of your wondrous deeds" (75:1). Now, in this continuation of the thought, the psalmist recounts some of those wondrous deeds.

It is an almost universal characteristic of people of Hebrew faith and descent to identify personally with the history of their ancestors. When one visits the Holy Land and a Jewish guide proudly points out historic landmarks, it is quite common for the guide to say, "It was here that we beat back the Greek invaders," or "It was at this place that we built a tunnel under the great wall, to bring fresh water into the city." Even though the events they describe occurred many centuries before they were born, they feel a personal identification with those events.

So the psalmist presents a list of historic achievements God had made possible for their ancestors, but which the psalmist claimed and cherished as though they had happened personally to him. "You really are an awesome God," the psalmist rejoices.

And what glorious gifts and blessings does the psalmist cite as the cause of his rejoicing? Not good physical health or a stock portfolio that shows a gain or a marriage that is functioning blissfully or children who are tractable and happy. No, the psalmist is rhapsodizing over the fact that God is God, and that God has shown strength in upholding the right and keeping the universe on the course for which it was created.

A little girl was praying her nighttime prayer, and she began a long list of requests for God to bless members of her family, her friends, her teachers and fellow students at school, her minister and Sunday school teacher, and assorted other people. Then, when she was almost finished, she added, "Oh, yes, God, bless yourself. Because if anything happened to you, we'd all be sunk!"

Through all the great catalog of God-inspired and empowered events that have blessed the world through the ages, every one of us has benefited. Ours is the victory of Moses and God over Egypt's pharaoh and the release of the Hebrew slaves. Ours is the rigorous discipline of the wilderness that prepared a people to establish a nation that would give birth to salvation. Ours is the drama of redemption, played out on the stages of human submission and divine intervention. Ours is the Bible, the church, and those saints, martyrs, priests, ministers, Sunday school teachers, and dedicated laypersons who through the centuries have kept the name of God in human currency and the wondrous deeds of God remembered.

Thank God for God! And thank God that every time God is offered a human heart as a starting point, every one of us is blessed.

DAY 77
Read Psalm 77

What spiritual misery is expressed in these words of doubt and despair! There is a hint of Jesus' cry of agony on the cross, in which he quoted Psalm 22: "My God, my God, why have you forsaken me?" The psalmist longs for the simple days of an earlier time, when God seemed so near and God's actions seemed so recognizable. The psalmist mourns the loss of such simple, childlike certitude. And who of us has not also grieved for the loss of childhood dogmatism?

Thomas Hood expressed this feeling in his poem "I Remember, I Remember." The last stanza says:

> I remember, I remember
> The fir trees, dark and high;
> I used to think their slender tops
> Were close against the sky.
> It was a childish ignorance,
> But now 'tis little joy
> To know I'm farther off from heav'n
> Than when I was a boy.

Somewhere along the road to spiritual maturity we have all suffered the loss of theological certainties that we once found so easy to accept. But such a coming of age is a necessary part of our spiritual growth. A kindergarten faith, untested in the real world of perils and evils, cannot suffice to arm and equip us for victorious living.

But the good news is that once we have come to terms with life's uncertainties and faith's reliance on our willingness to take that frightening "leap," we will find that the core of truth contained in our childhood dogmatism remains unshaken.

Karl Barth, the great theologian, was once asked by a student what was the most profound thought he had ever conceived. Without hesitation he replied, "Jesus loves me, this I know, for the Bible tells me so." He had made the successful journey from untested belief, through the pitfalls of doubt and danger, to discover that what he glimpsed through his eyes as a child was the same treasure he won at the end of his long and arduous journey.

Do you remember that vision you glimpsed as you set out on your journey of belief and discipleship? Cling to it, even if at times your experience seems to disprove its validity. The God you trusted in your childhood still watches over you.

DAY 78
Read Psalm 78

In this rather long psalm (second in length only to 119) we are given a history lesson about how God had protected, guided, and provided for the people of Israel. This was (and remains) a favorite theme of Hebrew teachers, who emphasize the truth that "those who do not remember history are condemned to repeat it."

Philosophers have recognized two kinds of human wisdom: the cumulative and the noncumulative. Some truths we do not have to learn for ourselves. We can profit from the lessons of those who went before us. We stand on their shoulders and can, therefore, see farther and benefit from their mistakes, as well as from their successes. But there are also noncumulative truths, lessons that every generation (or person) apparently must learn as though no one before had ever faced a similar experience. We do not have to learn for ourselves that fire burns. We can accept and profit from the painful experience of those who preceded us.

But the tragedy is that many people are not content to accept the wisdom of the past; they insist (to their sorrow) on learning for themselves the conclusions others have already drawn from cautionary events.

Imagine the boldness of trust required of the first Israelite who stepped down into the Red Sea *before* the waters began to recede! But for those who followed, it was simply a matter of accepting an already demonstrated truth: that when God calls us, God also provides for us a way to obey. And when the wilderness sojourners felt the pangs of hunger and saw no evidence of food to nourish them on their journey, it demanded heroic faith to believe God would somehow provide what they needed. Then the manna came to validate their faith, providing sufficient evidence for those who followed to trust in God.

But in subsequent generations the people forgot such evidences of providential care and demanded a current demonstration of God's willingness and ability to respond to human needs.

But lest we become guilty of "the pot calling the kettle black," let us be humble enough to recognize ourselves in the attitude of the perfidious Israelites. How many times must God answer our prayers before we stop accusing God of neglecting us? How many blessings must God heap into our grace-filled lives before we stop worrying about where tomorrow's bread will come from? All that we have seen of God should lead us to trust God for all that we have not seen.

DAY 79
Read Psalm 79

It is a sad irony that Jerusalem–the very name means "founded on peace"–has rarely known peace throughout its long history. Although its scanty patrimony of natural resources would not appear to make it an attractive target for conquerors or pillagers, there has not been a time in its long history when it has not been the scene of bitter warfare. Today it continues to bear the ugly scars of the wounds of hatred and ethnic rivalry. Jesus wept over the city, saying, "If you, even you, had only recognized on this day the things that make for peace! But now they are hidden from your eyes" (Luke 19:42). And the weeping continues.

Still, Jerusalem is also more beloved by a more diverse collection of human beings than any other city in the world. All three great monotheistic religions call it a holy city, and whatever the city may lack in beauty or concord or material wealth, it has a memory of the Divine at work in its midst. And it is that holy heritage that is the city's primary treasure.

"Here is where the Lord called Abraham to sacrifice his son," the tour guide says with pride. Or, "Here is where Jesus celebrated the Last Supper with his disciples." On a little hill just outside the city wall is a place made sacred by the blood of a suffering savior, and a few feet away is a grave in a garden, where the Christ is said to have broken the bonds of death.

In every nook and cranny of that city is something that stirs the reverent memory and gives evidence that God walked those narrow streets, rested beneath those trees, and entered that gate–not David, not Solomon, not even Jesus, but God: God's presence was once known in all those places, and where God has been, a halo of sacred significance remains.

Such is the power of the transforming God that anything–indeed, any one–God touches is forever changed. Like a plain wire grown incandescent, ordinary people have glowed like light bulbs when the light of the presence of the Almighty has been allowed to enter their lives. So that even when it is littered with the bleached bones and broken pillars of failure and sorrow, any city or any person who invites the Holy Presence to come in will be forever touched with beauty.

DAY 80
Read Psalm 80

Jesus may have had this lovely psalm in mind when, in the upper room, he told his disciples, "I am the true vine, and my Father is the vinegrower" (John 15:1). It was a metaphor with which residents of Israel would be familiar, for grapevines were grown in great abundance in the land. It was one of the few crops that could usually be depended on for bountiful harvests, if proper care had been taken of the vines. But if left unattended, the vines yielded little fruit.

So the psalmist sees the nation of Israel as a vine, brought out of Egypt and transplanted to a new location. First, the land had to be cleared, for the vine cannot thrive in competition with other vegetation. The land God gave the Israelites as a heritage had been overgrown with pagan tribes and barbarians, and they had to be banished from the land before the new nation of Israel could be planted.

In a classic Peanuts comic strip, Charlie Brown, with his incurable optimism, is preparing to celebrate the New Year. Lucy, grumpy as usual, asks, "New Year? What New Year?" Charlie Brown informs her that a brand new year is beginning. And Lucy replies, "That's impossible. I'm not through with the old year yet!" And most of us know exactly what she means. God tries to plant a new life in our hearts, but we are so clogged with memories of yesterday's mistakes and failures and sorrows that we have no opening in our lives to receive the gift.

But when God is invited to enter, a great clearance sale is held. It costs us something in terms of swallowing pride and letting go of lesser gods that have demanded our loyalty, but when we give them up, God clears a space for the vine of Christian discipleship to take root.

The vine of our discipleship is still God's, and it is subject to God's cultivating and pruning efforts. God cares for even our frailest efforts and patiently trains us in righteousness so that we may produce fruit for the kingdom of heaven.

And the vine God planted in Israel was destined, in centuries to come, to produce the fruit of salvation for humankind through Jesus Christ. He was "God with us." And Jesus' charge to us is to be the network of branches through which God will be known by the world. God planted you where you are. Bloom where you are planted!

Here the stage is set for a great celebration, and the whole symphony of praise is assembled. Along with the singing and the shouting, the timbrel, the lyre, the harp, and the trumpet all play their part in this "Hallelujah" chorus of thanksgiving to God. And for what is the psalmist offering praise? "I hear a voice I had not known," the writer says (v. 5). God had spoken in ways that had not always been recognized as the voice of God. "I relieved your shoulder of the burden," God reminds the people in verse 6, "your hands were freed from the basket," (or, you were released from the onerous labor of carrying containers full of bricks to the construction sites). But while they celebrated the gifts of such deliverance, they had not known that God was the deliverer. They saw the gift but not the giver.

Jean Webster's book *Daddy-Long-Legs* speaks of a girl in an orphanage who was befriended by a man who kept his identity unknown. A young bachelor, he was so charmed by this young girl that he maintained for her, across the years, a silent sponsorship. She once saw his shadow, cast from an open office door, and thought of him always afterward in terms of that elongated shadow across the floor: hence her name for him, Daddy-Long-Legs. And though she met the man often in person, she didn't realize that he was her benefactor. Up to the years of her maturity, her every need and favor and gift came to her by way of this someone in the shadows whose name she did not know. Of course, the story has a happy ending, a final scene, when she discovers the identity of her benefactor.

It is when that scene is missing that this romance resembles the tragedy of people whose lives have been supported, whose hearts have been nurtured, whose needs have been met, whose mistakes have been buttressed, and whose accomplishments have been made possible by someone in the shadows, whose voice they do not recognize.

As the popular writing "Footprints in the Sand" reminds us, we often realize, from the evidence we can see, that God has walked with us in the past—we can see those two sets of footprints side by side. But sometimes, in the worst times, we can see only one set of footprints. Yet that one set may not be of our own feet, struggling alone under our burdens. They may well be God's footprints—*carrying us*—though we did not recognize his presence at the time.

DAY 82
Read Psalm 82

This strange psalm cannot be understood in terms of our twenty-first-century perceptions. In several instances in the Old Testament, however, a "divine council," is spoken of, a holy court of heavenly beings who shared with Almighty God the responsibility and authority of judging the earth. Probably the most familiar of these references is in the book of Job, in which the "sons of God" sit with God in observing the earth and its inhabitants. Even Satan has a seat in this divine council, and it is through Satan's complaint against the special treatment God had given to Job that the story unfolds.

Is it possible that God does not occupy the heavenly throne completely alone? Remember that God is quoted, in the creation story, as saying, "Let *us* make humankind in *our* image" (Genesis 1:26, emphasis author's). And in a scene depicted in the book of Revelation, God's throne is surrounded by other thrones, one for each of twenty-four elders (Revelation 4:4). Seven angels are also described as being a part of the heavenly milieu. Maybe, as Marc Connelly quoted "De Lawd" as saying in *Green Pastures,* "Even bein' God ain't a bed of roses!" And perhaps God wants all the help available.

But despite such speculations, our God is the solitary creator, sustainer, and lover of all creation. No one cares as God does. No one suffers as God does. No one has the power to heal as God does. No one knows the meaning of the saying "Love not, sorrow not" as God does. No one assumes full responsibility for even the last and the least of the lost as God does. No one knows what every person needs as God does. No one has as soft a heart or as firm a demand for justice as God does.

Think of Jesus dealing with the sins of his contemporaries or the stupidity of his disciples. He did it alone. Think of Jesus praying in the garden of Gethsemane, facing a fork in the road at which he would choose to save himself or the world. He did it alone. Think of Jesus facing the cruelty of Herod and the apathy of Pilate and the blasphemy of the crowds. He did it alone. And think of him on the cross—alone!

However eager God's followers may be to help share the burden of righteous justice or compassionate ministry, God still faces the awful responsibility of *being God* quite alone!

DAY 83

In the first English translation of the Bible accomplished in the American colonies, the entire book of the Song of Solomon was omitted because, in the opinion of the straightlaced translators, the story it relates is entirely too earthy for consumption by Christians.

Similarly, when the *Liturgy of the Hours* was published by the Roman Catholic Church in 1971, three psalms were omitted because of the undertone of hatred and violence in them. This is one of them.

The psalmists were nothing if not realistic, and they recognized and reported the irrational but unrestrained vitriol that sometimes takes possession of us and makes us say things and do things that we would ordinarily go to great lengths to keep under control. But despite the demure reticence that pretends that we have no such ugliness buried somewhere in our makeup, the more candid of us will surely remember those times when some provocation sent us over the edge of our usual decorum, to fall headlong into the abyss of fury. Even Christian people get mad sometimes and "blow their stack." And if not exactly a crown of virtue, it is at least understandable, and forgivable.

Because anger comes so naturally to humans, perhaps we ought to find a way to direct it toward the proper targets and harness its power to make beneficial changes.

When Abraham Lincoln floated down the Mississippi River on a raft as a youth and visited the city of New Orleans, he saw in that city a slave auction. The obscene sight of human beings being sold like cattle gave rise to genuine anger in Lincoln. He later reported that when he saw it, he said, "If I ever get the chance, I'm going to hit that thing, and hit it hard." And he did.

When a young Canadian boy watched helplessly while his brother died of the mysterious illness of diabetes, that boy reacted angrily, condemning that thief of life and joy to the pursuit of his rage. And several years later that angry boy—now a grown-up Dr. Banning—introduced the insulin treatment that has saved millions of lives.

When Jesus entered the temple and found its holiness corrupted by dishonest merchants, he became angry and used physical violence to rid the temple of its malignancy.

The tragedy is that we are so easily angered by the superficial and so unruffled in the face of true evils. Perhaps it is time for us to examine Paul's advice: "Be angry but do not sin" (Ephesians 4:26).

DAY 84
Read Psalm 84

It was April 30, 1956, when Alben W. Barkley–"The Veep," as he was affectionately known–stood up to give a speech to an appreciative audience in Lexington, Virginia. He had been a popular political figure, having long served as a representative in the U.S. Congress and as a member of the senate, and finally as vice president under Harry S. Truman. An orator of the old school of political eloquence, he chose to conclude his speech with his favorite scripture. His resonant baritone voice intoned the phrases of the text: "I would rather be a doorkeeper in the house of the Lord than dwell in the tents of the wicked" (v. 10, paraphrase). The text had served him well, offering a kind of vindication for his satisfaction for serving always in a somewhat subservient role in government.

"The Veep" ended his speech with those ancient words and sat down. Within a few moments he was dead, with those favorite words still echoing against the walls of the chamber in which he spoke them.

Although few people would choose these words from Psalm 84 as their favorite scripture, there is no question that this entire psalm is one that the people of God have taken to their hearts. "How lovely is your dwelling place," it begins. How blessed are those who consciously dwell in the presence of God! Though the psalmist surely intended these words to refer to the temple, we can see in them the peace and joy that have been experienced through the ages by those who live day by day in the knowledge that they are surrounded by the grace of God. It is not a *place,* but a state of intimate closeness with the presence of the Lord in which we find this spiritual ecstasy.

But it is not sufficient for the psalmist to enjoy this state of spiritual bliss. It is an experience too good not to share. "I would rather be a doorkeeper" in the presence of God than to achieve the power and privilege that the world can give. A gatekeeper provides entry into God's presence. And those whose lives serve as a point of access to God's presence are twice blest.

Are there those who came to see God, to know God, and to dwell in God's eternal presence because of you? If you are a door, do you bring them in, or keep them out?

DAY 85
Read Psalm 85

The word *revive* means "restore to life," or "bring to consciousness." Its use in verse 6 implies a lesser state of existence prior to the action of God. Only God can give life and only God can restore life once it has been lost.

The psalmist links together the cause and effect of the faithfulness of God's people. They had displeased God, and they suffered for it. Sometimes there is a great lapse of time between the cause and the effect of our faithfulness to God, or lack of it. Sometimes it appears that there is no connection at all. Bad things do happen to good people, and the wicked do prosper sometimes. Many thousands of individual parts may go into the construction of a cruise ship. Most of those parts, taken by themselves, would not stay afloat. But put together, they remain on top of the waves. So not all the elements of life may be favorable, but when they are all put together according to God's purpose, they result in a viable existence.

God does not settle all accounts by Saturday afternoon, and the effects of our faithfulness to God may be long delayed. But God is, after all, the ruler of the universe, and God has built into the universe the principle that what is right and good will ultimately prevail, and what is wrong and bad will eventually fail.

But there is hope, even for those whose infidelity has disappointed God. A prominent preacher once published a sermon in which he referred to God as "The Lord of Second Chances." And there is limited truth in that statement, for God is also the Lord of third, and fourth, and ninety-second chances. And however foolishly we pursue less-than-righteous lives, and however tragic the consequences of our sin, God has both the power and the determination to restore us to life again–to give us another chance at life.

"Then Peter came and said to [Jesus], 'Lord, if another member of the church sins against me, how often should I forgive? As many as seven times?' Jesus said to him, 'Not seven times, but, I tell you, seventy-seven times'" (Matthew 18:21–22). If Jesus expected that unlimited mercy from us, can we not expect at least as much from God?

DAY 86
Read Psalm 86

If, as the heading of this psalm informs us, this is a prayer of David, one cannot help but be struck by the claim with which it begins, "for I am poor and needy" (v. 1b). Although there was not a person on earth at that time who could begin to count the immeasurable riches we have come to expect today as our "basic human right," David was surely in the highest bracket for income tax purposes. The fact that income tax was not a concern in David's time served only to increase his wealth.

But as many another "rich" man has discovered in a moment of terrifying clarity, this world's riches cannot provide protection against the alarms and vicissitudes to which all human flesh is heir.

A persistent legend–never documented in print–maintains that Mrs. Cornelius Vanderbilt, one of the world's richest women, was on the Titanic on that fateful night when it struck an iceberg. Mrs. Vanderbilt went to her staterooms and collected all the diamond jewelry she had brought aboard. But as she ran to the lifeboat, she realized how impotent such currency would be in this extreme emergency. At the last minute she returned to her stateroom and left the diamonds and picked up instead a bag of oranges. And with the nourishment of those oranges, she and her fellow lifeboat passengers survived the most horrifying experience of their lives. In that crisis she found herself as "poor and needy" as the most impoverished passenger in steerage.

With what currency will you confront the most grievous crises and alarms that may lie on the road ahead of you? And with what assets will you approach the Day of Judgment? No matter what blessings of riches and prosperity we may or may not have received, we will still be, like David, "poor and needy" when life's ultimate realities confront us.

To compensate for that essential poverty, David reached for a dependable treasure: his faith in God. Twice in this psalm David repeats the attribute of God that he saw as his hedge against the uncertain future: "abounding in steadfast love" (vv. 5, 15). *Abounding* means "overflowing" or "plentiful." God gives us more than enough of everything we need to fill our "poor and needy" lives with confidence and joy.

And such a treasure, David says, is available to all who call on God.

DAY 87
Read Psalm 87

A familiar hymn by John Newton takes its title and theme from this psalm:

Glorious things of thee are spoken,
Zion, city of our God.

Jerusalem has been called a holy city by all three of the world's great monotheistic religions. Unfortunately, it has never really deserved the name *Jerusalem,* which means "a city with a foundation of peace." Every inch of the city has been fought over fiercely, again and again, through the ages. It does not have a strategic location; it is not adjacent to a major body of water; it has no rich stores of natural resources; it is not on the road to anywhere. Its history is bloody, and it has lacked a stable government for almost all the centuries of its existence. Its sole asset seems to be its memory, but that is enough. When people visit Jerusalem, they do so to walk in the footsteps of Jesus, or David, or Muhammad, and to remember what those men did while there. And it is in the recollection of those events that our own faith is formed and strengthened.

A legend tells of Zacchaeus, the little man who climbed up into a sycamore tree to catch a glimpse of Jesus as he passed. Years after that event, the wife of Zacchaeus became disturbed by her husband's bizarre behavior. Every morning he would leave his house, but instead of heading toward his place of business, he would go in the opposite direction with a watering can in his hand. One morning, prompted by her curiosity, she followed her husband. As she hid behind a tree, she watched him approach the old sycamore that had been the place of his meeting with the Christ. He carefully swept the leaves and rubble away from its trunk. Then he poured water on the tree's roots, and with a smile of satisfaction on his face he patted the trunk of the tree and said over and over, "I met him here. Here is where I met *him.*"

Every Christian needs to have his or her own sycamore tree–a place or event hallowed by faith and sentiment–where he or she first came to know God. It may be a city–as Jerusalem is for many people. Or it may be a little country church where you first made your commitment to Christ. Or it may be an occasion such as a birthday or an anniversary of a spiritual milestone. But we need to revisit such landmarks frequently and find our faith renewed and our commitment strengthened by the experience. "I met him here," we may say of such a place. "Here is where I met *him.*" No more glorious thing can be spoken of any place.

DAY 88
Read Psalm 88

Among all the psalms of lament, this one is the most desperate. It arises from the pain and loneliness of a night of peril and despair. It may recall for us a similar time of wrestling with unmanageable troubles and seemingly hopeless situations. "The night has a thousand eyes," a poet has said, and it is when the darkness overwhelms us that we see ghosts of possible disasters that flee before the light of dawn. Can the Lord see us when it is dark, and does God care?

Grace Noll Crowell has written of a similar experience of struggling with the frightening apparitions of potential cataclysms and what we may do about it:

> Lord, it is dark; the road is rough to go.
> I lift an unlit candle in the night.
> Behold it, Lord, within my upraised hand.
> Touch it to flame with thine own heavenly light.
> This slender, waxen thing that is my faith:
> Fire it, Lord, with some divine white spark,
> Until its circle, widening at my feet,
> Will mark my certain way across the dark.
> Thou wilt light my candle: thus assured,
> I shall go forward through this unknown land.
> The way can never grow too dark, too long,
> For I shall bear thy light within my hand.

"This slender, waxen thing that is my faith" seems so fragile and impotent in the face of such monumental troubles as we face. But when we lift up that candle of faith to the presence of God, we find that God will put the light of divine strength and confidence in our hand.

A certain man of God was thrown into a dungeon, where he awaited execution the next day because of his faith. During the long night before he was scheduled to be burned at the stake, his confidence began to fail him, and he cried out, "Lord, give me grace to bear the fire!" But in the dark silence, he seemed to hear the word of God assuring him, "No, tonight I'm giving you grace to bear the fear. Tomorrow I will give you grace to bear the fire."

Even in the darkest night, God comes to us and gives us what we need: comfort for the night, and the promise of courage when daylight comes to conquer whatever we will face then.

DAY 89
Read Psalm 89

A common pattern in Psalms begins with a cry of despair, then works through the painful circumstances that had produced the despair, and ends with a note either of ultimate triumph or the confidence that God will bring the faithful ones to victory. Here, in Psalm 89, the order is reversed. It begins with one of the most brilliant and beautiful sections of praise to God to be found anywhere in scripture. Juxtaposed with the previous psalm ("my soul is full of troubles, and my life draws near to Sheol" [Psalm 88:3]) and reading straight on through the beginning of this psalm, the reader experiences a most abrupt shift in mood. It is almost like driving for a long distance in a dark tunnel and suddenly emerging into the brilliance of a sunny day.

Unfortunately, the mood changes toward the middle and end of the psalm and concludes with the desolate question, "LORD, where is your steadfast love of old?"(v. 49).

It is likely that this psalm was written to be performed at a royal function, probably during the reign of King David. It is carefully crafted to conform to a dramatic script, perhaps to be read while actors (or musicians) provided the interpretive music or pantomime.

First comes the prologue, invoking the blessing of God on the reign of David ("You said, 'I have made a covenant with my chosen one, I have sworn to my servant David: "I will establish your descendants forever, and build your throne for all generations'" [vv. 3–4]). It was like an obsequious salute to the king before the performance.

Then in Act I the glories of the past are celebrated: Israel had been faithful to God, and God had responded by providing abundantly for them and delivering them from their enemies ("For you are the glory of their strength; by your favor our horn is exalted" [v. 17]). Less exuberant is the reflection on the then-current reign of David in Act II. Although God still honors the covenant with the king, the relationship has become less than exciting to the king, who has found other pursuits to interest him and other comforts to give him solace.

Finally, Act III follows the downward spiral of the emotional and spiritual descent to the inevitable pit of destruction and despair. The collapse of the throne of David is depicted as the inevitable result of the dwindling of the faith of the people and their leader.

Such is the biography of many people–and many nations–who have begun with faith but ended with failure. Faith, like anything living, must grow, or it will die.

DAY 90
Read Psalm 90

Majestic Psalm 90 stands as one of the masterpieces of human literature, easily transcending both the time and the circumstances that produced it. It begins with an expression of wonder at God's eternal nature, in contrast to the fleeting span of human life. How can a God who framed the mountains and set the sun and stars in their courses have time and interest for those of us who are here for so brief a period and whose few days are filled with failure and trouble?

But such an astonishing fact is reiterated not only here but elsewhere in Psalms. ("What are human beings that you are mindful of them, mortals that you care for them?" marvels the writer of Psalm 8 [8:4].) It is a truth that we do not so much understand or accept but celebrate.

Such knowledge brings the psalmist to plead for the pity that we cannot deserve but on which we nonetheless depend.

At the conclusion of the psalm, there is a petition that asks God's participation in our own anemic efforts: "Let the favor of the Lord our God be upon us, and prosper for us the work of our hands—O prosper the work of our hands!" (v. 17). Surely God does not need us and is not depending on the frail efforts we make to share in the divine labors of the Almighty! But ironically, the majestic and eternal God wants our partnership and crowns it with grace.

Sir Hubert Herkomer was one of Britain's most prominent sculptors in a previous generation. At the time he was reaching his zenith as an artist, his father—also a sculptor—was losing his skill. His dwindling eyesight and feeble fingers could no longer produce the works of art that he had once created. To provide him some continuing activity, the son would often bring his father some modeling clay, to while away his evenings in the practice of his craft. But his declining faculties would no longer allow him to create any masterpieces, and the old man would go to bed quite sad. When he was asleep, the son would go to work on the clay, and with a few strokes would produce a masterpiece. The next morning the father would look at his work of the previous evening and, never knowing that another hand had touched it, would exclaim with delight, "Why, it's not as bad as I thought!"

So we offer our pitiful efforts to God. They are not what we wanted and certainly not what God deserved. But they are the best we can do. And when we give them to God, something wonderful happens: God touches our work with the beauty of divine favor, and the result thus established blesses both our hands and God.

DAY 91
Read Psalm 91

Lutheran Pastor Reuben Gornitzka related an experience that occurred in his church during a Good Friday service. The mocking and torture of Jesus were dramatically reported in his Holy Week message, and the crucifixion scene was vividly described. But neither the pastor nor the other worshipers could ignore the sobbing of a little boy, sitting near the front of the nave. Finally his mother, sitting next to the boy, hushed his sobs with her admonition, "Don't take it so personally!"

Although the boy was, perhaps, a bit too young to be given such a large dose of reality, it is tragically true that many adults have learned not to take God's costly love personally. Such a filter of apathy has often kept us from knowing exactly how "personally" God expects us to take the story of redemptive love.

Psalm 91 must be taken not only personally but *intimately* if we are to understand it properly. It speaks of a caring God who takes us under a heavenly wing to protect us from danger and trials of a thousand kinds. It employs the imagery of guardian angels who watch us and guide our footsteps, and it makes quite clear the concept that God not only knows us each by name and by need but cares for us, quite as though we were the only lamb of God's flock.

Then the voice and mood change, and we are given, at the end of the psalm, a most astounding picture of God, saying the most amazingly comforting words about each of us that we can imagine. Hear God say this about you:

> Those who love me, I will deliver;
> I will protect those who know my name.
> When they call to me, I will answer them;
> I will be with them in trouble,
> I will rescue them and honor them.
> With long life I will satisfy them,
> and show them my salvation. (vv. 14–16)

Those words you can take to the bank. What's more, you can take them quite personally.

DAY 92
Read Psalm 92

A made-for-television movie delineated the adventures of a group of travelers on a package tour. It was one of those tours that attempted to do too much in too short a time, giving the travelers a glimpse of fourteen different airports in twelve days. On such a whirlwind tour, names and faces and places begin to blend into a blur, and the title of the movie might have been the exclamation of one of the confused tourists: "If This Is Tuesday, It Must Be Belgium!"

We are weary travelers, too, and our whirlwind rounds of daily activities and interests blur in our minds; we tend to forget where we are and what it's supposed to be like where we are. But when Sunday comes, we need to lift our heads and observe the landmarks and conclude, "If this is Sunday, it must be heaven!"

Such is the spirit of Psalm 92, which is identified in the heading as "A Song for the Sabbath Day." Radiant joy emanates from the lilting phrases of the song and surely denotes the kind of spirit that the people of God felt when the weekly Sabbath observance came along. In those hardscrabble days, when everyone worked to the point of exhaustion, the sabbath day came as a blessed relief. The families gathered together in their homes and ate special foods and experienced the joy of being with one another and with God.

Through the centuries, the Lord's Day—Sunday—has continued to be an island of blessing in the landscape of secular frustrations, for those who let that day bring them closer to heaven. In eighteenth- and nineteenth-century America, Sunday was kept inviolably as a day of rest and worship. Christians looked forward to Sunday, not only because of its respite from labor but also because the joys they experienced at worship were the most heavenly blessings of their lives. John Newton celebrated these Sabbath joys in his hymn "Safely through Another Week":

> Safely through another week God has brought us on our way;
> Let us now a blessing seek, waiting in his courts today;
> Day of all the week the best, emblem of eternal rest.

When we allow the Lord's Day to become just another day of business and busyness, we cheat ourselves of one of the gifts God has given us for the enrichment of life. If Sunday is not the joyous experience for you that it is supposed to be, then you're missing a special blessing. What you do on the Lord's Day should evoke from your grateful heart the spirit that says, "If this is Sunday, it must be heaven."

DAY 93
Read Psalm 93

An amateur sailor brought his sailboat near the shore for the night. It was a perfectly windless night, and the sea was as smooth and still as a sheet of glass. Surely on such a night it would be unnecessary to go to the trouble of anchoring the ship. So he joined his wife belowdecks for a few hours of sleep. But during the night the winds returned and stirred the sea into a churning caldron that sent the anchorless ship drifting far from shore. When morning came, the skipper came up on deck and, seeing the trackless ocean on all sides, shouted to his wife, "We're not here anymore!"

It is disconcerting to find ourselves in a world that contains few landmarks that we remember from our youth. Something has happened to our world, and we don't like it.

A small detail in Washington Irving's story of Rip Van Winkle illustrates our frustration. Before his twenty-year nap, old Rip had enjoyed consorting with friends at the King George Tavern. But after his long sleep, he returned to his village and saw that the tavern was now known as the President George Tavern. A whole revolution had taken place, and he missed it.

So many revolutions are taking place in our world, some of which we hail as progress and others of which frighten us by destroying or undermining the landmarks that we once depended on to give us direction. We know what the sailor meant when he said, "We're not here anymore!"

In such times when we fear for the future of our world, we need to be reminded of the statement from this psalm that the Lord "has established the world; it shall never be moved" (v. 1). *Established* means permanent. And what gives our world its permanence is the fact that a God who is likewise permanent established it. "He's got the whole world in his hands," the song asserts. "You are from everlasting," the psalmist says (v. 2); "your decrees are very sure" (v. 5). And neither nuclear weapons nor fanatic terrorists nor human stupidity can wrench the world out of God's hand. As Paul later declared: "For I am convinced that neither death, nor life, nor angels, nor rulers, nor things present, nor things to come, nor powers, nor height, nor depth, nor anything else in all creation, will be able to separate us from the love of God in Christ Jesus our Lord" (Romans 8:38–39).

A popular speaker revealed that he kept on his desk a snow globe paperweight. Inside the paperweight there sits a little man. And when that paperweight is shaken up, snow and clouds swirl around and obscure the little man inside the globe. The speaker said that when his own world is shaken up by frightening or disturbing events, he takes that paperweight into his hands and says, "Little man, you are disturbed; you are all shook up; your world is all cloudy, and you can't see clearly right now. But I want to assure you that I hold you right here in my hand. Your whole world is in my hand, and I'm strong enough to hold you." The speaker said he then just sits quietly and holds the weight very still, and the clouds settle and the blizzard subsides, and the atmosphere around the little man clears. Then he says to the man in the globe, "You see, little man, you didn't have anything to worry about. I was here all along."

Do you feel like that little man inside the globe sometimes? Frightening events and ghosts of possible calamities ahead swirl around us; our vision is dimmed; and when we cannot see any farther than the end of our nose, we obsess over our own predicament and the perils we fear we may later face.

In such a time of confusion and doubt, sometimes we even turn on God and accuse God of not tending to business. "Rise up, O judge of the earth; give to the proud what they deserve!" (v. 2). ("Wake up, Lord, and tend to business! Have you left the monkeys in charge of the zoo?")

Then another voice is heard. Is it the voice of God answering the complaint? Or is this the other side in an internal dialog within the mind of the psalmist? We do not know who speaks up in God's defense here, but the logic is unassailable. "If you think God doesn't see what's going on around you, you are mistaken. The God who made eyes and ears can surely see and hear."

And if it seems to you, little man or little woman, that the ungodly are getting all the goodies and winning all the games, perhaps you are blinded by the swirl of fears and events now surrounding you. Maybe you need to hear again one of the most difficult commandments to obey: "Be still, and know that I am God!" (Psalm 46:10).

DAY 95

Twice in the opening verses of this psalm we are enjoined to "sing" in praise to our God. Twice more the command is to "make a joyful noise," which offers some comfort to those of us whose singing voice may be something less than lyrical.

To be sure, there are times when we don't feel like singing. In their Babylonian captivity, the Israelites found themselves in a situation in which singing didn't seem appropriate. "How could we sing the LORD's song in a foreign land?" they asked (Psalm 137:4). But singing praises to God is not the result of taking an inventory of things for which we can be glad. It is the paean of praise that even when we are in unfavorable circumstances, God gives us something to sing about.

And often that ability to sing makes a witness to those around us. When Paul and Silas were in prison in Philippi, life must have seemed cruel and hopeless. Their anthem might well have been "Nobody Knows the Trouble I've Seen." But we are told that "about midnight Paul and Silas were praying and singing hymns to God." And in a striking phrase, the record states that "the prisoners were listening to them" (Acts 16:25). What a witness that simple act of worship must have made to the hardened jailer, who was surely more accustomed to hearing curses from the captives than hymns! Shortly thereafter we read that the jailer confessed his faith in Christ and asked to be baptized.

Surely their "songs at midnight" made more of an impression than any arguments they might have put forth.

In Robert Browning's poem "Pippa Passes," he told of a young girl who toiled day after day at her menial job. Once a year she was given a day off, to spend as she pleased. On that day, instead of pouring out her complaint at the injustice of life, she went through the city lifting up her lilting voice in a song:

Morning's at seven; the hillside's dew-pearled...
God's in his heaven; all's right with the world.

Her little song of simple trust, sent innocently into the environment, had a most remarkable effect on those who heard it. People who were engaged in—or plotting—some devilment were touched by her song and repented of their evil. Although she was completely unaware of it, her song became a powerful witness.

And if we know that God is in heaven, then we have something to sing about.

DAY 96
Read Psalm 96

What's this? In the midst of one of the Old Testament's most lyrical and beautiful songs of praise to God, almost like a crass and impudent interruption of the majestic images of a lofty worship experience, comes the injunction, "Bring an offering" (v. 8). What a letdown!

But the offering we bring to God is as much a part of our worship as the songs and the scripture readings.

At a small country church, a pious elder was serving as liturgist. He distributed the offering plates to the waiting ushers, and before sending them forth to gather the tithes and offerings from the congregation, he prayed this simple prayer to God: "Lord, no matter what we say or do, *this* is what we think of you."

A young man was pouring out his romantic feelings in a love letter he was writing to his sweetheart. He waxed eloquent in the words, "I would swim the deepest ocean to spend one moment with you. I would climb the highest mountain to be in your presence. I would walk through fire to see one of your smiles." Then in a postscript he added, "I'll be over Saturday evening if it doesn't rain."

Strange, isn't it, how the genuineness of our love is confirmed or denied by our willingness to "put our money where our mouth is"? God is not honored by empty phrases and eloquent words, but by a practical and day-by-day demonstration, in terms that prove our commitment, that God is worth more to us than our money. Jesus said of the hypocritical Pharisees, "This people honors me with their lips, but their hearts are far from me" (Matthew 15:8).

In churches on the American frontier, many years ago, it was the custom for the men to leave their guns at the door. This was done not to preserve the peaceful sanctity of the place, but simply because they did not want to subject their guns to the Christian teaching against violence. They would not bring their guns to the altar of God, because when they left their worship experience, they wanted to be free to use their guns again without the restraint the Christian ethic might have placed on them.

It is for that same reason that some people leave their money at home when they go to worship. They don't want their money tainted by the warning of Jesus that "you cannot serve God and wealth" (Matthew 6:24).

But those who really love God and wish to express it in their worship bring their money with them. "Bring an offering!"

DAY 97
Read Psalm 97

Like a scarlet thread in a woven tapestry, there is one theme that finds expression again and again in Psalms. It is the realization that our God is Lord of all the earth.

"Let the earth rejoice"(v. 1), not just that small corner of the earth occupied by the Israelites.

"Let the many coastlands be glad!" (v. 1). "All the peoples behold his glory" (v. 6).

We must remember that at that time the Hebrews believed that they, and they alone, were the people of God. They were an island of truth and reverence in the midst of a sea of evil and paganism. Their word for "foreigner" and the word for "heathen" were the same word.

But still they could not entirely escape the understanding that God claimed all people as his beloved children. Some people do not know that yet, and some have forgotten it. Some don't want to know it, and some may know it but refuse to acknowledge it. But God regards every person on this planet as a beloved child. And God loves them all.

It can be very comforting to us to know that God loves us, but sometimes it comes as a great shock to us to learn that God loves other people just as much as God loves us. God loves the devout and the deviate, the pious and the impious, the saint and the sinner, with the same astonishing devotion. God loves Pope John Paul II and Osama bin Laden, Billy Graham and Charles Manson, with the same astonishing devotion as his son demonstrated on Calvary.

And the frightening conclusion we are forced, by this knowledge, to concede is that if our God loves them, we must find some way to love them, too.

Donald Westlake tells of a woman whose house was being picketed by angry militants during one of the ugly riots of the 1960s. She spent those hours in her house preparing lemonade for the picketers. Apparently she had heard it from someone that she ought to love her enemies. We have heard it too. We have heard it from the lips of no less than the Son of God, who loved even those who hammered the nails in his hands and prayed for their forgiveness. They, too—as brutal as they were, and as determined as they were to take God's most precious gift to the world and drag it through the muck of shame and the blood of pain—they, too, were children of God, and Jesus loved them anyway.

It is a gloriously difficult thing for us to put into some kind of practice. But it is a truth we cannot escape: God is God over all the earth and all its peoples.

DAY 98
Read Psalm 98

This so-called enthronement psalm is one of several that were intended for use at special festival occasions. In many respects it conforms to the other similar writings. But there is one small detail that gives this psalm a special meaning. Whereas other songs of praise include instructions for the use of musical instruments (such as Psalm 150, in which seven different instruments are invited to join the song of praise), this is the only one that includes a reference to "the sound of the horn"(v. 6).

The horn referred to would be the ram's horn, or shofar, which was ordinarily used only on the Jewish New Year, or the Day of Atonement. In that festival one sheep or goat was selected for sacrifice, and the sins of all the people were confessed over it. Then the animal was sacrificed, or sometimes only beaten and scourged and released into the wilderness to die. In the death of that "scapegoat," the sins that had been consigned to it died as well, thus giving the people a fresh, new, unblemished beginning.

Some scholars believe that it was from this sacrificed animal that the horn was removed, and when a priest blew that horn, it was a signal to the people that their new life could begin.

Even today the ram's horn is blown in Jewish celebrations, to notify the people that their sins are forgiven and they may start a new life.

This psalm, then, was probably reserved for use on that high and holy day, which signified God's forgiveness and mercy.

The offering of animal sacrifices ended with the destruction of the temple. But both Jewish and Christian people recognize the need for "wiping the slate clean," now and then, to claim the opportunity to make a fresh start.

We need not wait for a special occasion or make a specific sacrifice to obtain such a blessing. As Paul said, "For our paschal lamb, Christ, has been sacrificed. Therefore, let us celebrate" (1 Corinthians 5:7–8).

By the grace of Jesus Christ, any day can be a day of atonement; any day can be the end of a sinful chapter of our lives and the beginning of a new one.

Do you hear that horn blowing right now?

Three times in this psalm the Lord is described as "holy" ("Holy is he," in verse 3, and again "Holy is he" in verse 5, and finally "for the LORD our God is holy," in verse 9). The Hebrew word thus translated is *qadosh,* which has the root meaning of "separate" or "completely apart" from all else. Karl Barth, the great neo-orthodox theologian, referred to the Lord as "the wholly other." Isaiah heard God declaring his "separateness" in his words, "To whom will you liken me and make me equal, and compare me, as though we were alike?" (Isaiah 46:5).

God is absolutely and utterly unique. Unique in power, in righteousness, and in love, God is in a category in which no other being exists. There are no words in our dictionary that can describe God, so we must resort to what God *isn't.* God is immortal, we say (not subject to death). God is invisible (not seen). God is unchangeable, and unconquerable, and incorruptible. "As the heavens are high above the earth, so great is his steadfast love" (Psalm 103:11).

But wonder of wonders! This heaven-high, incorruptible, immeasurable God is willing to condescend from that immensity to woo us into the eternal kingdom in which God alone is fit to dwell. Little wonder we celebrate the "God-with-us" event that we call Christmas. God's astonishing intention in that miraculous event was set forth by the prophet Hosea: "I am God and no mortal, the Holy One in your midst" (Hosea 11:9).

What emotion and response such a realization should evoke from us! Recently the President of the United States made an unannounced visit to the home of a family whose farm had been ravaged by spring floods. Imagine the panic of the family members.

But the holy God is present in your home, even as you read these words. What preparations have you made, and with what courtesies of honor and reverence will you welcome that guest? Often seen in homes a generation ago was a framed postulate that said:

Christ is the head of this house,
The silent listener to every conversation, and
An unseen guest at every meal.

How do you live knowing that the Holy One is present with you?

DAY 100
Read Psalm 100

"Old Hundredth" is the name we give to the paraphrase of this psalm set to music that we call "The Doxology," and which is sung Sunday by Sunday in most of our churches. It is the psalm that is read more often at Thanksgiving time than any other.

Its majestic phrases roll off the tongue so blithely that we frequently forget the richness of the meaning the words convey.

Central in the psalm is the reminder of who God is ("Know that the LORD is God" [v. 3]), then cast into that knowledge is the encouraging affirmation of who we are: "It is he that made us, and we are his; we are his people, and the sheep of his pasture" (v. 3).

Many a Christian parent has utilized a simple cautionary reminder to their children as they leave the house to go beyond the watchful care of the parents: "Remember who you are." It should also be added, "and remember *whose* you are." For, as the apostle Paul pointed out, "you are not your own...you were bought with a price" (1 Corinthians 6:19–20).

When Harry Truman was president, an attempt was made on his life by a misguided terrorist. When the attempted assassin was apprehended, the police, who suspected that he was a member of a foreign conspiracy, interrogated him. "What do you belong to?" they asked again and again. Finally the unhappy assailant replied, "I belong to no one, and I suffer."

There are many people today who are suffering for lack of a meaningful relationship, and as a result, they do not know who they are. And though their disconnectedness does not often push them to such extremes of antisocial behavior, they, too, suffer.

A little boy, the son of the director of development for a benevolent home, overheard his father anxiously reporting to his wife that he had been given the responsibility of raising a million dollars for a new building to house the elderly. The lad, thinking he would help with that gigantic effort, went to the doors of his neighbors to ask for donations. One neighbor asked why he was collecting funds. He said, "I'm raising a million dollars to build a home for old people." When the neighbor remarked that it was a rather sizable task for so small a lad, the boy replied, "Oh, I'm not doing it by myself. My little brother is across the street, and he's helping me."

When you feel overwhelmed by the burdens life has imposed on you, remember that you're not in this alone. You are a child of God, and God will help you.

DAY 101
Read Psalm 101

"The light that shines farthest shines brightest at home," runs an old axiom. And it is true. No amount of religion in the temple will save us if we do not also practice that religion in our own homes, where we rub shoulders daily with those whom God has given us as our primary congregation.

It is this thought that David expresses in the words, "I will walk with integrity of heart within my house" (v. 2). It is often true, however, that we are much less likely to express and demonstrate our Christian faith at home than anywhere else. Outside the home, we are the soul of courtesy to others, even to total strangers on the street who stop us to ask directions. But at home the thin veneer of civility wears off, and we are impatient and brusque with members of our own family. A fragment of an old poem accuses us:

We save for our own the bitter tone,
Though we love our own the best.

Few of us will ever make a greater contribution to the world than what we accomplish in our own homes, in producing children who will bring gifts of strength, integrity, and sensitivity to those around them.

John's gospel reports that when Andrew and John met Jesus, they were attracted to his teaching, but before they enrolled as his disciples, they went to spend a day with Jesus in his own home. And it was what they saw of him there, in the familiar surroundings of his daily life at home, that convinced them that Jesus was the Messiah.

How long would it take people, visiting in your home, to conclude from what they saw of you in your own house, amid the members of your own family, that you are a Christian?

One of the principal ingredients of David's "integrity in his own house," is also reported: "I will not set before my eyes anything that is base" (v. 3). Those words reach down more than thirty centuries to find a greater application than was true in David's day. Think of what we set before our eyes, which are fixed on the television screen. How much that is base do we permit to enter our homes and silently and insidiously mold our character? Surely walking "with integrity of heart in my house" involves keeping guard against the base things that seek to enter our eyes and our ears.

It is quite clear, from the rich imagery utilized in this writing, that the psalmist was suffering a major illness. The symptoms of that illness are reported, almost as if in speaking to a physician to seek a diagnosis and a cure. He complains of a fever ("my bones burn like a furnace" [v. 3]), a loss of appetite ("I am too wasted to eat my bread" [v. 4]), the resulting weight loss ("my bones cling to my skin" [v. 5]), heart trouble ("my heart is…withered like grass" [v. 4]), and a persistent fear that his death is drawing near, even at so early an age ("he has broken my strength in midcourse" [v. 23]). In such a serious illness, he wonders if he is going to die in middle age ("O my God…do not take me away at the mid-point of my life" [v. 24]).

Perhaps a modern physician could analyze the symptoms and make a diagnosis. But whatever the malady, the fact is that here was one who was suffering a serious illness and brought that ordeal to his God in prayer.

It comes as no surprise to us that good people, even righteous people, do go through times of illness and suffering. And Jesus spent much of his time and energy helping to alleviate the pains of the people. It will not do to spiritualize the complaints that people brought to Jesus and to assume that he was interested only in the souls of the people. Their bodies, too, were temples of the Holy Spirit, and being well, or "whole," as Jesus often referred to it, is within the will of God for all of us.

Perhaps one day science will discover the root cause of all the many ailments that afflict us. But even now our doctors warn us that we bring on many of our own illnesses by our stress (which denotes a lack of trust in God) and by our overindulgence, which is making a god of our bellies, as Paul defined gluttony in his letter to the Philippians (3:19). Anger, too, plays a demonstrable part in many of our illnesses.

But whatever the illness—whether physically, spiritually, or emotionally generated—it is not what God wants for us, and it is the holy intention that we should be released from our illness. Therefore, it is right and good that we should bring our complaint to the Great Physician. Often a healing comes from that act of trust.

But whether the body is brought closer to perfect health, our whole lives are brought closer to God. And that is healing, indeed.

Until the coming of Christ into the world, this graceful psalm was the best picture of God's astonishing grace available to a world hungry for good news. It repeatedly speaks of the steadfast love of God and offers several striking illustrations of how that divine attribute expresses itself in the lives of those who know God and have experienced God's benevolent interventions.

"As the heavens are high above the earth, so great is his steadfast love toward those who fear him" (v. 11) is one of those efforts to express the infinite in finite terms. How high is heaven? Even with the most powerful telescopes, one cannot measure the distance between earth and heaven. "As far as the east is from the west, so far he removes our transgressions from us" (v. 12). Just how far is it from east to west? Neither attempt to measure the extent of God's love in human terms even hints at the magnificent truth of God's passionate and infinite concern for us.

"What language shall I borrow," asked Bernard of Clairvaux, "to thank thee, dearest Friend?" All our finest efforts to describe such grace are beggared by the task. All we can do is accept it—humbly and gratefully—and live a life that expresses that gratitude.

What does such knowledge evoke from us? Surely nothing we own or can do will repay God for this amazing grace. But at the very least—poor as we are—we can open our lives and pour out all that we are and have in tribute to God. "Let all that is within me bless his holy name."

"All that is within me"? We are such mixed bags of good and bad. What could God possibly want that we have? What God wants from us is nothing less than everything! But even when our everything is pitifully meager, it is enough to open for us the floodgates of God's mercy.

Ah, yes! The cost to us seems great. But see what we receive in return. When we give all that we are and have to God, God pays us the magnificent favor of giving us, in return, all that is God's to give, even the sacrificial offering of the Child of God, who gave all that was within him to show us, beyond all doubt, how much we are loved by the Ruler of the Universe.

DAY 104
Read Psalm 104

It has been called "the newest old hymn of the church"–"How Great Thou Art."

Although both the words and the music have roots in Swedish folk culture, the hymn was not written until 1953. Made popular by George Beverly Shea, of the Billy Graham organization, this hymn by Stuart K. Hine expresses the same thought as majestic Psalm 104. Both the hymn and the poem discern the fingerprint of God on all creation by considering the creative works of God:

> O Lord my God! when I in awesome wonder
> consider all the worlds thy hands have made,
> I see the stars, I hear the rolling thunder,
> thy power throughout the universe displayed.

And after this first stanza, and each of the rest that follow, is the refrain: "How Great Thou Art!"

In the same spirit, but in much more detail, the psalm finds in the universe proof of God's power and providential concern. From the heavens above (stretched out "like a tent" [v. 2]) to the stability of the earth ("set...on its foundations, so that it shall never be shaken" [v. 5]), God's great power is demonstrated. But God is defined not only in such huge considerations but also in each tiny detail of creation, such as the grass, which the Lord planted in order for the cattle to have something to eat. In both the minute and the vast, God's astonishing power and dependable care may be seen.

A book was published a few years ago with the intriguing title *Between an Atom and a Star.* The premise of the book was that human beings are as much larger–proportionately–than an atom as a star is larger than a human being. As such, we stand right in the middle of God's scheme of creation. And if God cares about each atom and tenderly guides every star in the heavens, we may be assured that we also enjoy that providential care God lavishes on us. "Living things both small and great," the psalmist says, "all look to you" (vv. 25, 27).

A generation or so ago, in devout but depression-poor homes, a word of faith was often quoted by people who didn't know where their next meal was coming from: "The Lord will provide." And although human failures have often impaired the delivery system, the Creator has put into our world what everyone needs. Both power and providential care are in the essence of God. God is great, and God is good.

DAY 105
Read Psalm 105

Our hymnals contain many references to "the story": "I Love to Tell the Story," "Tell Me the Old, Old Story," and "We've a Story to Tell to the Nations," to name but a few. The fact is that the people of God have a story to tell, and it is both our joy and our responsibility to tell it.

Psalm 105 is a poetic recitation of Israel's story. It traces the purpose of God through the destinies of the Hebrew people from Abraham, Isaac, and Jacob through the miseries of their bondage in Egypt and their release from it. Then there follows an account of the sojourn in the wilderness, with God's careful provision for their needs, then the conquest of their promised land and their occupation and settlement of it. Surely this psalm was used not only to teach children the history of their people but also to remind their elders of it.

But see what the bottom line of this psalm reports was the divine purpose behind all this history: "that they might keep his statutes and observe his laws" (v. 45).

It is well for us to remember that people came to the shores of America in the first place not so they could do what they wanted, but so they could do what God wanted them to do. It was the same purpose that gave energy and direction to the development of the Hebrew nation: that they might keep God's statutes and observe God's laws.

We Christians also have a story to tell, and a primary focus of our attention, when we gather to worship, is to remember and retell our story. Our sharing of the eucharistic sacrament is a way of rehearsing the story and imprinting it ever more indelibly on our consciousness. And what is the purpose of this frequent retelling? It is to remind us that God has given us a new life, not so we can do what we want, but so we can do what God wants.

An old chestnut of a story pictures three little boys boasting about the work of their fathers. One said, "My daddy is a doctor, and I can be healthy for nothing." The second said, "My daddy is a teacher, and I can be smart for nothing." The third said, "My daddy is a minister, and I can be good for nothing."

But it was not "for nothing" that God called us into the kingdom. It was for a divine purpose, and that purpose is so that we will be able to obey God's laws and fulfill God's hopes for the earth.

For what purpose did God send the Christ to bring you to redemption? Is your life fulfilling that purpose?

DAY 106
Read Psalm 106

This psalm, which seems at first glance to be a reiteration of the history recorded in the previous psalm, is really the underside of God's dealings with Israel. In the last psalm, there is rejoicing in the recollection of God's wonderful works in leading and providing for the people of Israel. Psalm 106 reports the faulty—and often shameful—response of the people to these divine mercies.

It is clear from verses 46 and 47 that this psalm came out of a time in which the people of Israel were in bondage ("He caused them to be pitied by all who held them captive" [v. 46]) and in exile ("Save us, O Lord our God, and gather us from among the nations" [v. 47]). In all probability the captivity referred to had occurred after the fall of Jerusalem, almost six centuries before Christ, when many of those who had lived in Jerusalem were brought to Babylon to live as slaves.

It was, therefore, in sorrow that the psalmist remembered the mercies of God and the people's rebellious response to those evidences of God's grace.

It has been said that we can live in such a way as to reap either results or consequences. And each of us makes that choice. But often it is not until we are suffering the consequences that we gain the wisdom to discern that such a repercussion proceeded from our own ignorance, stupidity, or defiance.

An old Pennsylvania Dutch axiom says, "Ve grow too soon oldt, undt too late shmart." Although experience may be the best teacher, we should not have to experience all the tragic consequences of wrong deeds to know which lifestyle will bring happiness to ourselves and others and which way of living sows the seeds of destructiveness. We can learn from the mistakes of others and from the seasoned wisdom of the Bible, as well as from the wisdom that accrues from our daily walk with God, which paths to avoid and which to follow.

But every generation in history has had to learn certain sad truths for itself, and the same is true for every person. However pious and faithful our parents or grandparents may have been, we cannot claim their righteousness for our own. Each of us must "work out [our] own salvation with fear and trembling" (Philippians 2:12).

DAY 107
Read Psalm 107

"This is my story, this is my song, praising my Savior all the day long." So runs the refrain of Fanny Crosby's loved hymn "Blessed Assurance." Her story was such good news that it had to express itself in a song. It became the theme song of her life and work.

So the psalmist had a story to tell, and in the telling of it, each episode called forth the thematic refrain, "Let them thank the LORD for his steadfast love, for his wonderful works to humankind" (vv. 8, 15, 21, 31). No doubt the frequent repetition not only made a witness to those who were listening (or reading), but also kept the psalmist in constant remembrance of the state of amazing grace in which he or she lived.

Do you have a theme song? Many people of faith have chosen a hymn to represent their own religious experience, and have memorized its words, and have sung (or repeated) the words at frequent intervals, to provide a spiritual mantra to strengthen and renew their faith. If you haven't yet chosen a hymn, it might be an excellent spiritual experience for you to sit down with a hymnal and leaf through its pages, reading all the words of several stanzas. In all probability your search will be rewarded with a felicitous discovery— a hymn that may well serve as "the theme song" of your faith and life.

It has been said that every hymn in the hymnal was produced by someone's deeply felt religious experience. And although not all hymns speak in the same way to everyone, there are many jewels yet to be mined from that great storehouse of faith.

Corrie Ten Boom related the true story of a young girl who was thrown into a Nazi prison because her Christian faith prompted her to help save her Jewish friends from the terrors of the Holocaust. In that prison she was in the company of many rough and crude men. But during that long ordeal she held on to her faith with the help of her favorite hymn, which she sang aloud several times a day:

When peace, like a river, attendeth my way,
when sorrows like sea billows roll;
whatever my lot, thou hast taught me to say,
it is well, it is well with my soul.
                    (Horatio G. Spafford)

And it was in the singing of that theme song of her life that she found the strength to endure through her ordeal and to bring a fresh glow of grace to a very dark place.

DAY 108
Read Psalm 108

In the *King James Version* of this psalm we read the opening words, "My heart is fixed." Although the *New Revised Standard Version* selects the word *steadfast* to help us to understand the intended meaning of the word *fixed,* the older translation provides a play on words that gives us an explanation of how our hearts can be made "steadfast." In the modern vernacular the word *fixed* is utilized to mean "repaired" or "reconstructed." And the fact is that many people feel rootless and unsettled because their hearts have been broken. Some disappointment or sorrow has robbed them of the spiritual security that would provide the steadfastness that would give us peace. Our hearts need to be "fixed," or made new.

There is a saying that, for all its simplicity, speaks a dependable truth: "God can mend a broken heart if we give God all the pieces." And it is only when we have given the Creator our fragmented lives that re-creation can begin. "If anyone is in Christ, there is a new creation: everything old has passed away; see, everything has become new!" (2 Corinthians 5:17).

At other times our hearts are out of order because we have invested them in the wrong things. Our hearts are set on things that we should not want. Even Paul recognized that in his past he was a walking civil war, part of him wanting what the rest of him hated. Who could "fix" such an out-of-order heart? "Who can deliver me?" he cried in anguish. But the answer came in his surrender to Christ, who alone could restore wholeness to his conflicted heart.

The writer of Ephesians urged us to grow up in every way, so that we might not be "tossed to and fro and blown about by every wind of doctrine" (Ephesians 4:14).

Sometimes our spiritual groundlessness results from the fact that we have not leaned our whole weight on God, but have allowed our doubts and uncertainties to rob us of the peace that results only from our complete trust. Sidney Lanier, in his poem "The Marshes of Glynn," wrote:

As the marsh hen secretly builds on the watery sod,
Behold, I will build me a nest on the greatness of God...
By so many roots as the marsh grass sends in the sod,
I will heartily lay me ahold on the greatness of God.

And what serenity comes when we let go, and let God fix our hearts!

DAY 109
Read Psalm 109

It is ironic that the writer of this psalm begins by reporting the pain he had suffered as the result of cruel words spoken by enemies; then, in subsequent lines, the writer invokes some of the most merciless curses on these enemies one can imagine.

It grieves us to recognize that David, to whom the psalm is attributed, could be capable of such hurtful words, particularly in view of the fact that many of his other Psalms were so affirming and encouraging. That paradox should warn us that we might often be guilty of the same behavior we despise in others.

The fact is that words may convey both blessings and curses, and, if the words of Jesus are to be believed, we will be held accountable for what we say. He said, "I tell you, on the day of judgment you will have to give an account for every careless word you utter; for by your words you will be justified, and by your words you will be condemned" (Matthew 12:36–37).

In earlier times we had a whole arsenal of offensive weapons by which we could oppose our enemies. But in our more civil day, the number of weapons in our arsenal has been reduced to one: our power of speech.

How it hurts us when gossiping tongues slander us—especially when the slander is true! When we are falsely accused, we do have, at least, the truth on our side. But when the defamation is true, we have no defense.

But what magnificent mercy is demonstrated when one who seems to have a perfect justification for condemnation withholds the criticism. Think of Jesus, when the self-righteous Pharisees threw a sinful woman indignantly at his feet. Jesus knew what she was and what she had done. He might have lectured her sternly and reminded her that she had brought her censure upon herself. Instead he won her heart (and the heart of all humankind) by withholding his criticism, and offered her another chance at a more reputable life. Who can doubt that his words to her became messengers of mercy? And if the woman in that story was Mary Magdalene, as many scholars believe, think of the treasure of inspiration that resulted when a kind and encouraging word created a saint!

"A word fitly spoken," says the proverb, "is like apples of gold in a setting of silver" (Proverbs 25:11). If you know of a word that would result in such a blessing for someone, for the sake of your soul—and theirs—say it!

DAY 110
Read Psalm 110

Psalm 110 is more often quoted in the New Testament than any other Old Testament writing. It was generally regarded as a messianic prophecy that was perfectly fulfilled in the person of Jesus Christ. The apostle Peter was the first to voice that belief, when he quoted the scripture in his sermon on Pentecost (Acts 2:34–35). Additional references to the picture of Jesus being seated at the right hand of the throne of God may be found elsewhere in Acts, 1 Peter, and Revelation.

The image of being seated at the right hand of one in power was familiar to people of Bible times. Even today books of etiquette insist that the most honored guest at a dinner is to be seated at the right hand of the host. It was a sign of favor and respect. This psalm, which was probably used as a part of a coronation ceremony for a king, begins, "The LORD says to my lord, 'Sit at my right hand'" (v. 1). The confusion of the two "Lord" references is made clear when we learn that the first "Lord" refers to God; the "small-l" lord specifies the king being crowned. "My Lord God Jehovah says to my king, 'Sit at my right hand.'" What a frightening sense of responsibility such words must have given the newly crowned king. Imagine being given both the honor and the chilling obligation of being "at God's right hand." But it was the belief, in Old Testament times, that civil authorities derived their power from a special relationship with God. Would that even today our governmental leaders might understand their role of leadership as representing the justice and righteousness of God!

But as a messianic prophecy, the psalm tells us much about Christ's role as the mediator between God and the human family. He represents us at the throne of grace, just as Christ represented God to us. "In Christ God was reconciling the world to God's self" (2 Corinthians 5:19).

One of the privileges of the "right hand" favor was that the one so honored had the opportunity to speak privately to the one in power and to intercede on behalf of people of his concern. That is one of the most magnificent understandings we may grasp regarding the position of Christ at God's throne. He has promised to pray for us, to guide us, to protect us, and to reward our faithfulness. And when your name comes up in the divine court of justice, what a joy for us to remember that Christ—your beloved friend—is right there, speaking on your behalf to a listening God.

DAY 111
Read Psalm 111

The line "The fear of the LORD is the beginning of wisdom" (v. 10) was probably a familiar saying of the day, since it was incorporated not only in this psalm but also in Proverbs 1:7, with the slight change of *wisdom* to *knowledge* in Proverbs. In either case, the "fear of the Lord" is the place where it all begins.

Timid translators have often shied away from the use of the word *fear*, sometimes substituting *reverence* or *respect*, neither of which captures the full extent of the meaning of *fear* as it is used in the Bible.

To fear the Lord is surely to recognize the awesome power of God (the psalmist chooses the word *terrible* to describe God's might). To disregard that power is the beginning of stupidity.

The power of gravity is astonishing, holding planets and stars in their places. But whereas gravity can be harnessed to provide blessings for humankind, ignoring that power can be a deadly folly. Gravity serves us when it brings drinking water into our homes from a reservoir or water tower, but it curses us when we ignore its irresistible claim and try to rebel against it by jumping off a cliff, expecting that we may prove to be an exception to that inviolable rule. One would be a poor airplane pilot, indeed, if one did not accept and respect the power of gravity.

So God may be—and usually is—the most benevolent power in the universe, and millions of people have been blessed by that beneficence. But God may also be a fearful enemy to everything evil and to everyone who espouses that evil.

The writer of Hebrews shocks us with the statement that "it is a fearful thing to fall into the hands of the living God" (Hebrews 10:31). Too often people think of the Christian life as being like a children's birthday party, where everybody wins and everybody gets a prize. But at the heart of the Christian faith is the ever-present though often-neglected reminder that there is a consequence to our sin. We cannot continue forever to insult God and trivialize the holy laws without coming some day to the staggering realization that God will not—cannot—smile indulgently at our petty impiety and our blasé apathy.

Wisdom is a complex and wonderful achievement, and every person may have a unique share of it. But it always begins with recognition that there is no god but God. And ignoring that truth is the beginning of self-delusion.

DAY 112
Read Psalm 112

This psalm, like the one immediately preceding it, is an acrostic, with the first word in each line beginning with a letter of the Hebrew alphabet in sequence. The subject of the psalm is the blessed life of a man of God. Like Psalm 1, this psalm provides a template for the life that is lived by people who "fear" the Lord and live by God's commandments.

There is an interesting difference in this psalm, however: It depicts the dark and difficult world in which this good man must live. It is a world of darkness (v. 4), in which bad news is commonplace (v. 7). There is hostility in this world (v. 8), and there are wicked people who make life difficult for those who would be righteous. But the man or woman of God will endure these ills and ultimately triumph over them.

A grade-school lad was playing his first game of football. At one point in the game he was told that the football would be passed to him, and his job was to carry the ball across the goal line. But that simple instruction proved to be a bit difficult, because, as the boy later complained, "I tried to get it across the goal line, but people kept bumping into me!"

How easy it would be to live a Christian life if people who oppose us or ridicule us or hurt us were not constantly bumping into us. "In the world you face persecution," Jesus said to his disciples in the upper room (John 16:33). And he never said a truer word. Those early followers of Jesus faced persecution, defamation, imprisonment, and death as frighteningly real possibilities. All of them except John died a martyr's death.

Jesus added, "Take courage; I have conquered the world." But in those long stretches of difficulty and suffering between Jesus' promise and their reaping of that promised reward, they would have to live and do their work in a world that made even their holiest intentions an obstacle course of daily crises.

Do you sometimes feel that being a Christian is difficult and requires some real sacrifice on your part? Then rejoice! You are surely doing something right.

DAY 113
Read Psalm 113

A mother of ten children had been selected by the local newspaper as "mother of the year" and was being interviewed by a reporter. "Which of your children do you love the most?" the reporter asked, the ironic smile on his face a hint that he expected the honored mother to protest that she loved all her children the same. But she surprised him by replying, "I love most the one who's sick, until he's well, and the one who's away, until he's home."

Several years ago a bit of a rhubarb was stirred up over a religious leader's remark in a publicized address that "God is partial to the poor, the powerless, and the discriminated against." Some people objected, saying that the scripture makes it clear that God shows no partiality. God cares about the mighty and the humble, the righteous and the wicked, the rich and the poor, with the same passionate intensity.

But there is a sense in which God has a special concern for those people for whom nobody else cares. God "raises the poor from the dust, and lifts the needy from the ash heap," this psalm points out (v. 7). And who can doubt that even though God's mercy toward us is not mitigated by it, God does exhibit an extraordinary regard for people who seem to have fallen through the cracks of the world's solicitude.

This point is vividly demonstrated in Jesus' parable of the lost sheep (Luke 15:3–7). The gospel hymn says, "There were ninety-and-nine that lay safe in the fold," and it is ironic that we have formed our picture of that story of Jesus more on the basis of how an old hymn misinterprets it than what the Bible actually says. Leaving ninety-nine safe in the fold to find the one lost is one thing. But it is quite a different thing to hear the word of scripture that insists that the shepherd left the ninety-nine *in the wilderness,* where they were far from safety, and still subject to getting lost, stolen, or eaten by marauding animals.

If we think with the mind of Christ, we will cherish every human being on the face of the earth, whatever that person's race or gender or nationality or moral or spiritual or political status. In other religions there are castes, outsiders and insiders, the unclean, the untouchables, the worthless infidels, those destined by fate to be slaves and nobodies. And if there is anybody on this earth who is loved less or cared for less than God wants a child of the Divine to be, God will find a way to exhibit special care for that one. And if you are the one through whom God demonstrates that special care for those in special need, you will share in that blessing of extraordinary grace.

Read Psalm 114

The lyrical images of this psalm describe the odyssey of the Israelites from their release in Egypt to their settlement in Israel. How delightful is the poetry that says, "The [Red] Sea looked and fled...[and] the mountains skipped like rams" (vv. 3–4). Celebrated in this poetry is the fact that God cleared a path by which the Israelites could respond to God and accomplish the divine destiny. And, indeed, poetry seems a more suitable genre of communication than dry-as-dust history to report the kind of adventure God and God's people shared in the wilderness.

It seems to be a rule of nature that when we live "with the grain" of the universe, we get results; when we live against the grain of the universe, we get consequences, every time.

In Old Testament history, Sisera was an evil figure. He was commander of a Canaanite army that held Israel captive for some time. But he found—tragically too late—that opposing what God wants done is to invite the whole universe to conspire to defeat you. In Judges 5:20 it says, "The stars...from their courses...fought against Sisera."

When we are doing what God wants done, God will not suffer our efforts to fail. But if we seek to accomplish what God does not want, or if we attempt to frustrate what God does want, we will find ourselves facing a whole concatenated army of adversaries pitted against us. And every person creates his or her own universe, in which the stars are kindly or hostile, and the mountains terrifying obstacles or friendly as skipping rams.

What makes the universe friendly or hostile to us depends, of course, on our relationship with the Creator. If we know and love God, we will find the creation as benevolent as its Creator.

A little boy was sleeping alone in his bedroom when a storm shook the earth with its thunder and lit it up with brilliant flashes of lightning. His mother, thinking the lad might be frightened by the storm, went into his bedroom, to find him standing up in his bed, smiling in the radiance of the lightning. "Oh, look, Mama," he said with delight, "God is taking my picture!"

Knowing God, and feeling loved by the Creator, turned a menacing universe into a friendly one. It happens to adults, too!

It is obvious, from this writing, that Israel was suffering humiliation at the hands of its pagan neighbors. "Where is their God?" the pagans demand to know (v. 2). And many a more recent believer has been nagged by doubts when God did not come through with the help needed at the time needed it. "Where are you when I need you?" the anguished believer reproaches heaven.

But although God's ways are unsearchable and often incomprehensible, we know that our God is at least capable of response, unlike the pagan idols who have eyes but cannot see, ears but cannot hear, and mouths but cannot speak. How can we expect something made with our own hands to come to our aid?

The picture is reminiscent of the irony of Isaiah (Isaiah 44:9–20), who pictures a man cutting down a large tree. With part of it he makes a fire to warm himself. With another portion of the tree he makes a fire to cook food for himself. As the trunk of the tree becomes smaller and smaller, more and more mundane uses are found for it, until at last there is only a small residue left. And with that leftover kindling he makes an idol and falls down before it, beseeching, "Save me, for you are my god!" (v. 17).

That old text has been useful to many generations of Christian preachers, who have seen it as a cautionary tale underlining the danger of giving God only the leftovers of our time, our money, and our affections. What we give to God increases God's ability to work in our lives! But there is a flaw in that conclusion, and it is this: No matter how generously—even sacrificially—we may give to our God, what we render to God does not make God any more capable of or willing to answer our prayers.

This caveat has an important message for people who look at religiously motivated extremists and conclude that their sacrificial worship must somehow empower their false religion to give them a pass to heaven. Or, at least, a god who can inspire such a martyrdom must ipso facto be a true god.

But God is not proved by any betrayal of the will and nature of God. Only God is God, and nothing we may do can make God any more or less than God is.

DAY 116
Read Psalm 116

The Shakers, whose simple lifestyle gave credence to the belief they claimed, had a song that has become an American classic. It says:

> 'Tis the gift to be simple, 'tis the gift to be free,
> 'tis the gift to come down where we ought to be,
> and when we find ourselves in the place just right,
> 'twill be in the valley of love and delight.
> When true simplicity is gained,
> to bow and to bend we shan't be ashamed,
> to turn, turn will be our delight
> till by turning, turning we come 'round right.

Such was the spirit of the psalmist as he recalled a time of grievous illness that brought him near death. But when he was brought low, "the LORD [protected] the simple" (v. 6).

In the midst of the rich panoply of diverse worship styles and experiences by which modern Christians praise God, sometimes we wonder if, for all their beauty and stimulation, they may have led us to think God wants such grandeur or excitement from us. But although worship is essential, as the source of the motive power that fuels our discipleship, God has insisted that a simple life of humility, trust, and service is more to be desired. "He has told you, O mortal, what is good; and what does the LORD require of you but to do justice, and to love kindness, and to walk humbly with your God?" (Micah 6:8).

Amos heard God saying to the religious establishment of his day, "I hate, I despise your festivals, and I take no delight in your solemn assemblies" (Amos 5:21). What God wanted from the people was a simple lifestyle that honored God and served the people.

An American churchwoman was visiting India on a vacation and asked to visit the home of the missionary her church sponsored. She was gladly welcomed into that home, but she was puzzled by its emptiness. "But where is your furniture?" she asked. He turned the question back on her, "But where is your furniture?" "Oh," she replied, "I'm only passing through." The missionary replied, "And so am I."

The Lord protects the simple.

DAY 117
Read Psalm 117

Not only is this the shortest of the Psalms, it is also the shortest chapter of the entire Bible. In only two verses, or a total of twenty-nine words in our translation of the Bible, it proclaims one of the biggest thoughts to be found in holy writ. "Praise the LORD, all you nations!" it begins. "Extol God, all you peoples" (v. 1). Here is the reminder of the mature realization of the Hebrew people that our God is everyone's God.

When the apostle Paul sought to prove that God's love embraced all people of all nations, he quoted this verse (Romans 15:11). As acceptable as this truth may be to us, it was a dramatically different picture of God than was the most common view in the time in which it was written. We must recall that to most of the Hebrew people of the age, there was a kind of exclusive relationship between themselves and God. If they were God's chosen people, they reasoned, that meant that God had chosen all others to be outside that relationship. Their word for "foreigner" and the word for "heathen" was the same.

But in the call to worship represented by this psalm, the doors were opened wide, and the welcome mat was put out for all people.

An old hymn expresses it in these words:

There's a wideness in God's mercy like the wideness of the sea;
there's a kindness in God's justice, which is more than liberty.
For the love of God is broader than the measure of our mind;
and the heart of the Eternal is most wonderfully kind.
(Frederick W. Faber)

A Christian missionary in China reported that a young man in his Bible class, whose name was Lo, came to him one day with exciting news to report. "The Bible has my name in it," he said, "and it says that God will always be with me!" The missionary asked where in his Bible he found such a personal assurance. "Here it is," he said, pointing proudly to Matthew 28:20 in his *King James Version:* "'Lo, I am with you alway, even unto the end of the world.'"

And no matter what your name is, or where you live, or the circumstances of life you face, you can put your name in that scripture, for Christ is with *you* always.

DAY 118
Read Psalm 118

Someone whose study of the Bible tends toward the mathematical has computed that Psalm 118 is the middle chapter of the Bible, with as many chapters preceding it as following it. And in the midst of (if not exactly in the middle of) this psalm is the much-loved bidding, "This is the day that the LORD has made; let us rejoice and be glad in it" (v. 24).

Although the placement of that cherished verse is only of incidental importance, it may be used to express a most heartening fact. Each of us has a past. Some of us have much to regret; others may have a great deal to recall with gratitude. For some of us the future is short and threatening; for others an endless string of promising tomorrows beckon invitingly. But right in the middle of our considerations for the past and the future is this one day: a present given us as a "present" by a generous and understanding God.

Someone has pointed out that yesterday is gone now and, however well or poorly we lived it, has passed beyond our reach. Tomorrow is not yet ours, and we have no rightful claim on it. All we really have is today. If ever we are going to accomplish anything important, it must be today. If ever we are going to speak an encouraging word to someone in distress, it must be today. If ever we are going to begin a good custom or break a bad habit, it will have to happen in the space between today's sunrise and this evening's nightfall.

For some people, today is a day of pain and sorrow; for others today will come to them bearing a cargo of happiness. But everyone's today comes with a celestial fingerprint: God's. It is the Lord of Creation who made this day and served it up to you, bearing all the gifts and promises you will need to make this day a real blessing to you and to those around you.

Today—whether it is the first of January or the thirteenth of March or the twenty-ninth of October—is a red-letter day. You are alive today; you have a measure of health and more material prosperity than most of the world's people. Today you have unique opportunities to make a contribution to the world you live in. And today you have a Redeemer who brings you into fellowship with the God of all good news. This is a day that was created to provide exactly what you need and want most. If you can't "rejoice and be glad" in a day like today, you must not be paying attention!

Not only is Psalm 119 prodigiously long (its 176 verses make it the longest chapter in the Bible by far), it is also a meticulously crafted literary masterpiece. It is divided into twenty-two "stanzas," each of which could stand alone as a wellspring of personal inspiration. But there is more evidence of the writer's methodical craft. Each of the twenty-two stanzas contains eight verses, and each of the verses starts (in the original Hebrew language in which it was written) with a letter of the alphabet, beginning with the first *(aleph)*. In the second stanza, each of the eight lines begins with the second letter of the alphabet *(bet)*, and the pattern continues through the Hebrew alphabet, to the last letter *(tav)*. Imagine the time and thought devoted to such a complex but flawless treasure of holy writ!

To give this psalm the attention it deserves, let us consider each stanza, giving us a full twenty-two reflections on this great work.

Although there is a central theme that holds all the stanzas together (the "law" or "precepts" of God's commandments), each section approaches it from a slightly different angle.

In the first section the writer prays for steadfastness in keeping God's law.

Ralph Waldo Emerson observed that "consistency is the hobgoblin of little minds." And although that may be somewhat true in some contexts, it is a far more valid observation that consistency is the necessary discipline of the committed.

God's laws are not suggestions, to be followed when it is convenient or pleasant to do so. Obedience brooks no compromise, permits no substitutes, allows no footnotes claiming exceptions. God's laws do not go out of fashion or allow amendments of human preference that negate the intent of the law. The truth is never to be found on a bargain counter.

A popular song of a few years ago presents a frivolous young man making a "fingers-crossed" promise to his sweetheart: "I will always be true to you, after my own fashion." But no spouse would accept such an insipid promise, and neither will God.

DAY 120
Read Psalm 119:9–16

In today's culture, many young people attach little importance to "keep[ing] their way pure" (v. 9). For that matter, most adults exhibit small concern for such a goal. But purity—in the sense of moral perfection—is not the point of this writing. "Pure" can also mean single-minded, or staying on track. It was in this understanding of the word that Jesus said, "Blessed are the pure in heart, for they will see God" (Matthew 5:8). William Barclay, the great Scottish scholar, translated that verse, "Blessed is the man whose motives are always entirely unmixed, for that man shall see God."

Young people today face unprecedented perils and temptations as they go out into a dangerous and confusing world. They hear voices from their peers, from television and movies, and from the lyrics of popular songs that seek to dissuade them from the path that would lead them to the fulfillment of their highest potential. What can they be given that will protect them from such distractions and ensure that they stay on the right road?

The psalm suggests that the answer is to be found in learning and remembering the Holy Word of God. There was a time when children and young people in Sunday school were given "memory verses," which they were encouraged to learn, to give them a treasure store of Christian teaching from which they could draw in times of confusion and doubt. To be sure, such rote learning of scripture was not always the best method of giving youth a solid foundation of religious truth. But it is as regrettable as it is unarguable that few young people today have in their moral armory such expressions of Christian teaching that will come to their minds in times of doubt or temptation, to encourage them to "stay on track" in their pursuit of a good life.

But whatever deficiency we may feel in this matter, it is not too late to begin to build and equip such a moral armory. Select a scripture of your own choosing today. Read it aloud several times until you have committed it to memory. Then as each day comes, say the scripture again. You will be surprised how many occasions may present themselves in which the scripture you learned will be appropriate and helpful. Then you will be able to say, with the psalmist, "I treasure your word in my heart, so that I may not sin against you" (v. 11).

With that gem of truth on deposit in your bank of memory, you can withdraw it whenever you need its inspiration.

Read Psalm 119:17–24

"I am a sojourner on earth," the psalmist observed (v. 19, RSV), and that is a discovery we all need to make. However long our span on the earth, it is an undisputable fact that the life we live here is not permanent. We are only "passing through." And although the earth may be pleasant, and the associations with others enjoyable, and the work we accomplish meaningful, we are only deluding ourselves when we suppose that such attractions are more than transitory.

In calling the roll of the biblical heroes, the author of the Hebrew epistle said of such luminaries as Abraham, Sarah, Isaac, and Jacob, "All of these died in faith without having received the promises, but from a distance they saw and greeted them. They confessed that they were strangers and foreigners on the earth" (Hebrews 11:13). And each of those people and all the others listed in that great Hall of Faith had this in common: They knew that the life we live here is not all there is. There is more to come. And until we have come to terms with that understanding, life here will always be frustrating and disillusioning.

Picture an astronaut leaving his space capsule to take a "space walk." He knows that he is temporarily occupying alien territory, in an environment that will not support his life. So he is careful to make sure that before he opens the hatch to venture into hostile space, he remains connected to his source of life by an "umbilical cord." That connection provides the oxygen-rich air that he can breathe and keeps him in communication with his associates in the capsule and even with those at the Johnson Space Center who are directing his activities in that unfriendly atmosphere. The umbilical cord also provides assurance that he will be able to find his way back to his space capsule and, eventually, back to his home and family.

So we are aliens in this world. Our bodies, coming from the earth, will share the destiny of all things earthly. But that of us which is really alive—our souls—came not from the earth, but from the hand of God. And God has "put eternity into man's mind" (Ecclesiastes 3:11, RSV). Our souls were not meant for eternal occupancy in this world, and when we realize that, we are released from many frivolous concerns. That understanding also prompts us to seek and maintain that communication with the other world in which our souls are native. And that spiritual umbilical cord is our contact with God. God speaks to us through the holy word; we speak to God through prayer. And with that continuing connection, we find an atmosphere in which our souls can live and thrive and in which we find "the way home" guaranteed.

Daleth is the fourth letter of the Hebrew alphabet, and in compliance with the established pattern of this psalm, the first letter of the first word of each line begins with that letter. Not only is that so, but the very theme of the psalm is "way," which, in Hebrew, is *derek,* which begins with the letter *daleth.* God's way is seen as the right way for a wise human being to live, and all other ways are false.

Having passed through a time of reaping the consequences of going the wrong way, the psalmist—wiser now, because of his painful experience—focuses his attention on the right way, and so eager is he to travel in that path that he does not speak of "walking" in the way of God, as so many other psalms do. Instead, he says, "I run the way of your commandments" (v. 32).

One of the Old Testament's most puzzling characters is Ahimaaz, who served as a messenger for his general, Joab. When entrusted with a message to be delivered, Ahimaaz would run with great speed until the message was delivered. One day, however, when the messenger reported for duty, Joab had no message for him to deliver. But he insisted on running with empty hands. Astonished, the general asked him, "Why will you run...seeing that you will have no...tidings?" Ahimaaz replied, "Come what may...I will run" (2 Samuel 18:20–23).

But running without tidings is always a waste, even in our day. It is so easy for us to mistake busyness for achievement and haste for proficiency. Hurry and worry are the twin offspring of the marriage of egotism and despair. Egotism says, "If I don't do it, it won't get done." Despair says, "If I fail, all fails." And they push us beyond our strength and past the point of our productiveness, until all that we have to boast of is an exhausted body and a depleted spirit.

But patience and confidence are the pacemakers that regulate our running. "Therefore," the writer of Hebrews wrote, "since we are surrounded by so great a cloud of witnesses...let us run with perseverance the race that is set before us, looking to Jesus" (Hebrews 12:1–2).

What is important is not how fast you run, or how far, but where it takes you.

Many people assume that the truths that comprise the Christian faith are so simple even a child can understand them completely, and that theology serves only as a pretentious obfuscation of that simplicity.

A theologian and an astronomer were seatmates on a plane. Upon learning of each other's vocation, the astronomer said, "Well, I guess you might say I'm a theologian, too. And my theology is 'Live and let live.'" The theologian replied, "I suppose you might say I'm an astronomer, too. And my astronomy is 'Twinkle, twinkle, little star.'"

No, although God has put the basic essence of the Christian faith within the reach of every seeking mind, we do not suddenly come into command of all the facets of our belief in a moment of inspiration. And learning about our faith is not only helpful but mandated.

"Study to shew thyself approved unto God," Paul wrote to Timothy (2 Timothy 2:15, KJV). And Jesus indicated that the most important of the commandments is this: "You shall love the Lord your God with all your heart, and with all your soul, and with all your mind" (Mark 12:30). And Peter urged, "Always be ready to make your defense to anyone who demands from you an accounting for the hope that is in you" (1 Peter 3:15). Could you do that? Could you properly defend and explain the Christian faith if such a demand were placed on you?

Someone remarked that it seems odd that people may be in a Sunday school class for fifty years and never graduate or feel prepared to teach someone else. Frank Laubach, the great literacy advocate, a few years ago insisted that one did not really learn until one confirmed one's learning by teaching it to someone else. His strategy for world literacy was "each one teach one." And that was Christ's plan for evangelizing the world.

In the twenty centuries since Christ gave us the Great Commission, in only two of those centuries have individual Christians been able to possess their own printed copy of the Bible. But those who do not read it have no real advantage over those who cannot read it.

God has provided all the resources we need for learning. We have the printed word; we have the example of Jesus Christ, the living word; we can hear the word read and explained in the church; and we can learn the truths of the Christian faith by the witness of the lives of other saints.

The obvious next step in your learning is to find someone to teach.

DAY 124
Read Psalm 119:41–48

It may be a bit difficult for us to comprehend the attitude of the Hebrew people toward the law. It is not enough to say they accepted it, or respected it, or obeyed it, though all those things are true. The astonishing thing about their feeling toward the law is that they had such great love for that collection of rules. In this psalm the writer declares, "I find my delight in your commandments, because I love them. I revere your commandments, which I love" (vv. 47–48). And often in Psalms there is a joyous outburst, "LORD, how I love your law!" Most of us feel a certain bit of resentment when any "thou shalt" or "thou shalt not" is imposed on us. And if we obey such a mandate, it is only because we know that, like medicine, it is good for us.

But the law represented far more than a code of moral and ethical conduct. It was the sign of the covenant between God and Israel. The law was a gift to the people, and it was understood as that. The people of Israel cherished the law because it was the way to covenant with God.

The Ten Commandments were inscribed on two stone tablets. We ordinarily think of each tablet as containing five of the commandments. Instead, scholars now believe the two tablets were two identical copies of the law. When a covenant was made in Old Testament times, each of the contracting parties received a copy of the contract. The people of Israel saw those two copies as evidence of the covenant that existed between themselves and God. And each of the covenanting parties had a copy.

So the people of Israel loved the law because it was their copy of the contract with God; it was evidence of their special relationship with God. It was proof that God loved them and would provide for them. The law was confirmation of God's promise to them. No wonder they loved the law!

It is for that same reason that we Christians feel such love for Jesus Christ. He is more than an admirable historical figure, more than the founder of the church, more than an exemplar of a useful and productive life, more than an inspiring interpreter of the truth. Jesus is our link with God, our "advocate with the Father" (1 John 2:1).

Christianity is not a religion of laws, or rituals, or standards of behavior. It is a religion of relationship. And Jesus Christ is the sign and seal of the covenant we have with God. No wonder we love our Jesus!

DAY 125
Read Psalm 119:49–56

This is the seventh stanza of the long 119th Psalm; it is identified as the *zayin,* or the seventh letter of the Hebrew alphabet. The first word of each of its eight lines begins with that letter. Three of the lines begin with the Hebrew word *zekor,* which may be translated "I remember" or "I do not forget." So in these words we are encouraged to remember, to keep in mind those things that will keep us faithful in our spiritual pilgrimage.

Quebec City is the oldest continuously existing city in North America and our continent's only walled city. The people are justly proud of their heritage, which makes them what they are. And the official motto of the province of Quebec reminds them of that. It's on the license plate of every vehicle on the street. It says, in French, *"Je Me Souviens."* "I Remember." What they are is what they remember. Their memory has forged their identity. And so has ours!

As the Hebrew people remember their release from their bondage in Egypt and their deliverance through the Red Sea on dry land, their holy memory brings them into covenant with God. And as they recall the days of deprivation and struggle, through the forty years of wandering in the wilderness, that recollection provides a template for the living of newer times, when the wilderness is more figurative but the spiritual dangers no easier to endure.

So as Christians we gather around a table at worship and share a simple meal to recreate a holy supper spread before other disciples many centuries ago. And as we eat and drink together, we recall the words of Jesus, who said, "Do this in remembrance of me" (Luke 22:19).

Remembering the landmarks on our spiritual pilgrimage renews and refreshes the spirit that infused us and empowered us to respond to God's call through Christ.

In the personal effects of a soldier killed in battle was found a paper on which he had inscribed a little prayer, perhaps the very day of his death. It said, "Lord, I will be very busy today. And if I should forget thee, please, Lord, don't forget me!"

That was all the penitent thief wanted when he cried to Jesus from his own cross, "Lord, remember me." And that is what Christ wants of us: "Remember me."

DAY 126
Read Psalm 119:57–64

"The LORD is my portion" (v. 57). At first glance this simple statement seems clear and easy to understand, but a closer look at the word *portion* gives us much to ponder. *Portion* means a part or a segment of the whole, an allotment or fragment. A secondary meaning is "apportionment" or "ration." But none of those synonyms seems appropriate as a definition of "the Lord."

But consider this: Every day—indeed every moment of every day—we are faced with choices that must be made. We are offered, in this world, a rich smorgasbord of opportunities and alternatives. And when we choose one option, we are thereby choosing to eschew all others. The very word *decide* has a root meaning of "to cut off."

"Forsaking all others," is the phrase used in the marriage ceremony to express this process of choosing an exclusive relationship with one person, thereby choosing not to consider the same kind of relationship with others.

An antique porcelain dish designed to be the receptacle for a wedding ring bears this legend:

My heart is fixed, it cannot range;
I like my choice too much to change.

In a faithful, loving, deeply committed marriage relationship, each has chosen the other as life's portion, excluding from that relationship all other persons and interests.

So in the spiritual life, we are called to choose to give our full allegiance to Christ.

In acknowledging that such an act is indeed a choice, we concede that other choices could have been made. One could choose another religion or no religion. Or one could choose a dilettante's middle ground of giving no one and nothing our whole heart.

But when with the psalmist we say, "The Lord is my portion," we are reporting that among all the endless options we might have considered, we have chosen the Lord as our life's portion.

Jesus recognized that process when he gently chided Martha for wearing herself out trying to prepare a complicated dinner to honor her holy guest, when she might have demonstrated a wiser choice, like Mary who, as Jesus said, "has chosen the good portion." (Luke 10:42, RSV). And as the familiar hymn points out, "When Jesus is my portion, my constant friend is he" (Civilla D. Martin, "His Eye Is on the Sparrow").

"We haven't said prayers at our house for a whole month," a lad boasted at recess one day, "and nothing has happened–" Then, with fingers crossed and a worried look on his face, he added the one word "–yet." As a matter of principle we believe that piety will result in a certain security and immunity from trouble. But as a matter of fact we have learned through disappointing experiences that such a consistent quid pro quo does not apply in this world. Neither good nor evil sows seeds that produce fruits in a single day.

And frequently often so much time elapses and so many events have occurred between seedtime and harvest that it is difficult to connect cause with effect.

The psalmist, however, felt sure that his perfidy has resulted in the ailment he was suffering. "Before I was humbled I went astray." (v. 67). And without doubt there was a logical rationale for his belief. Going astray is hazardous to one's health. But we must be careful not to distill an inflexible rule from so small a sample of human behavior. Bad things do happen to good people, and good things do happen to bad people. The psalms are replete with complaints that the righteous were suffering while the evildoers were "whooping it up" over their successes. But each of us is a mixed bag of good and bad, and as the old poem put it:

There's so much good in the worst of us
And so much bad in the best of us
That it hardly behooves any of us
To talk about the rest of us.

But little by little, moment by moment, day by day, year by year, we are gradually pursuing the kind of life that will inevitably result in blessing or bane.

But even the affliction-producing waywardness of the psalmist was not a complete loss. "It is good for me that I was humbled," he wrote, "so that I might learn your statutes" (v. 71). Even making mistakes can result in our blessing if we are humble enough to learn from them.

In a universe that reflects the character of the Creator, all things praise God–even mistakes that result in affliction that leads to repentance.

The first verse of this stanza begins with the declaration, "Your hands have made and fashioned me" (v. 73). The implication of the verses that follow is that because we are creations of God, what we are ought to reflect something of the character and identity of the Creator. Such a realization is further expressed in Psalm 139, in which the fourteenth verse claims, "I praise you, for I am fearfully and wonderfully made. Wonderful are your works; that I know very well." "I know this for sure," the writer declares. By looking at my own life, I can discern the hand of the Creator.

Is there, in your own life, some "chip-off-the-old-block" resemblance to the one who gave you life? Startling as such a statement might be, there is truth in it, and that truth is the source of the respect we should give our own lives.

The prophet Jeremiah heard the word of God directing him to go to the house of a potter and to learn a lesson from what he saw. As he watched, the potter made a beautiful vessel. But then something happened that spoiled the masterpiece that had been produced. Instead of throwing out the spoiled vessel, however, the potter worked carefully to restore it to its original perfection (Jeremiah 18:1–4).

The prophet saw this little episode as a parable of the history of Israel. God had called the nation of Israel into being and had demonstrated divine guidance, providence, and protection as the fledgling federation struggled toward nationhood. But wrong choices and stubborn acts of faithlessness marred the nation and sapped it of its divine power. The apostasy of the people resulted in a state that was vulnerable to the aggression of warring neighbors, and at the time of Jeremiah, little was left of the proud nation of Israel.

But there was hope for Israel, as Jeremiah reminded them that, appearances to the contrary, Israel could be reformed and restored, because what God created, God can re-create.

Listen: God has created you for sainthood! You were fearfully and wonderfully made by the very hands of God. And even though you may wander from the path of faithfulness, God has not given up on you. It is the will of God that you–being a creation of God–should bear the fingerprint of the Creator. Claim your inheritance!

"I have become like a wineskin in the smoke" (v. 83). This curious metaphor deserves a bit of examination. In the time of the psalmist's writing, wine was kept in pouches made from the skin of lambs or goats. When new wine was put into such a container, there was still enough elasticity in the skin that when the wine fermented and exuded gases, the wineskin was able to expand with the pressure. But when the wineskin got old, it lost its elasticity, and if fermenting wine was put into it, the brittle skin would burst.

In the arid climate of Israel, the useful life of a wineskin was greatly limited. Particularly if the skin was placed near a fire ("in the smoke"), it quickly lost its serviceability.

Jesus drew on this picture when he said, "Neither is new wine put into old wineskins; otherwise, the skins burst, and the wine is spilled" (Matthew 9:17).

So the psalmist was lamenting the fact that he had become brittle from disappointments and discouragement and could no longer contain the hope and joy that God had given him. Perhaps he failed to understand that God does not always behave in ways that our ancestors recognized as divine activity.

The nation of Israel had experienced God through their history and the Law that had been given them. Remembering their history and obeying the Law constituted their response to God. But when Jesus came, with his radically new message, the old wineskin of Israel's traditions could not contain it.

Perhaps the message for us is to keep our hearts and minds open to the new ways in which God may be working in today's world.

God may be speaking to us through new songs, new forms of worship, and new understandings of how the gospel expresses itself in human life. And such new experiences may stretch our wineskins of understanding and appreciation. But God does not always wave to us from the past. Rather, God's usual mode of communication is to beckon to us from the future.

Don't abhor the new just because it is new or revere the old simply because of its antiquity. Be open to God, ready to listen and respond to what God has to say to you today. Otherwise, you might become a wineskin in the smoke.

DAY 130
Read Psalm 119:89–96

It is not unusual for commercial enterprises to flatter their clients by issuing credit cards or addressing letters to "preferred customers." The implication is that since the customer has achieved this distinction by faithful patronage in the past, the company will repay such loyalty with special services or discounted prices. Being given priority over other customers strokes the swollen nerve of pride, and whether the touted distinction results in any measurable advantage, every person likes to think of himself or herself as deserving of such preferential treatment.

What would it be like to have this "preferred customer" distinction in our relationship with God? Surely having an intimate connection with the Almighty would suggest a magnificent array of favorable consequences, not entirely unlike the advantages enjoyed by "the boss's relatives."

It was this "preferred customer" status that the psalmist was counting on when he wrote, "I am yours; save me" (v. 94). Was it only empty arrogance that made him say that because he belonged to God, he had a right to ask God for rescue from his troubles? No, the psalmist was simply exercising the right God promised to those who acknowledge God's ownership.

There is a tender word spoken by God through the prophet Isaiah, in which the Lord says to the people, "Listen to me, O house of Jacob, all the remnant of the house of Israel, who have been borne by me from your birth, carried from the womb; even to your old age, I am God, even when you turn gray I will carry you. I have made, and I will bear; I will carry and will save" (Isaiah 46:3–4). What God has given life, God will protect. What God has created, God will carry. What God has loved, God will save.

You are indeed one of God's "preferred customers," with all the rights and privileges appertaining thereto. A hymn celebrates it:

I am thine, O Lord, I have heard thy voice,
and it told thy love to me;
but I long to rise in the arms of faith,
and be closer drawn to thee.

(Fanny Crosby)

So speaks the confidence of one who knows that he or she is a special child of God.

At first glance, this segment sounds like an immodest boast. Because of his diligence in reading and meditating on God's laws, the psalmist claims, he is wiser than his enemies, more understanding than his teachers, even more discerning than the aged, who were highly respected in biblical times for their sagacity. In fact, our irritation with such braggadocio makes us want to say, "If you're so smart, how come you're not rich?" Or, if the psalmist parades his wisdom and understanding so ostentatiously, why, in other psalms close to this one, does he complain of troubles and problems? With such acumen he could surely discover a way to solve the problems and avoid the troubles.

But one must believe that the psalmist did not intend his words to reflect favorably on himself, but to give glory to God. He was merely evidence of the soundness of the teachings that gave him the resources to live as he did.

And the validity of God's word remains unblemished, even after all these centuries. The Ten Commandments have sometimes been questioned, and often disobeyed, but never amended or rescinded. The whole system of laws in the Western world is based on the Ten Commandments. No one can claim to be intelligent or wise who does not know, or respect, or obey the Ten Commandments.

And the word of God, as revealed in Jesus Christ, remains the world's standard of moral, ethical, and spiritual conduct. Even those who decline to accept his lordship cannot fail to admire his teachings and his example.

A pretentious young man visited da Vinci's painting of the Lord's supper on the wall of the Santa Maria Della Grazie church in Milan, Italy. After spending a scant few minutes looking at the masterpiece, he remarked disparagingly to the nearby guard, "I don't think it's so great." The guard replied, "Young man, the picture is not on trial here."

So God's truth is not on trial. No one can really break God's laws. One can only break oneself upon them. When all its critics have died away, God's truth will remain inviolable. And when we know that, we have a wisdom that the world cannot deny.

DAY 132

If for no other reason, this stanza of the laboriously long 119th Psalm deserves our scrutiny because of the familiar verse with which it begins: "Your word is a lamp to my feet and a light to my path" (v. 105). The life of righteousness is compared here to a journey through the darkness. In the absence of streetlights, traveling at night was fraught with terror and peril. With no paved roads to travel, one had to beware of uncertainties underfoot and the threat of wild animals along the path. In addition, the darkness made it impossible to see far enough ahead to ensure that the travel would result in reaching the intended goal.

To ward against those twin perils, people often utilized two kinds of lamps. The first lamp, suspended on a chain or rope, illuminated the immediate condition of the road. The small circle of illumination was useful in avoiding such immediate hazards, so that the next step could be taken with some confidence.

But that foot lamp did not spread its illumination far enough ahead to ensure that the traveler was continuing in the direction that would lead to the desired goal. So a second lamp, held higher, was employed to bring some clarity to the more distant scene.

Neither lamp alone could provide all the illumination that was needed, but together they gave enough clarity to both the next step and the more distant goal to give a measure of confidence to the traveler.

So, the psalmist says, the word of God helps us walk safely, step by step, and also keeps the intended destination in focus. And in both those functions, the word of God keeps us safely on track.

One cannot give attention to the immediate without remembering the ultimate. And our focus on the ultimate fails if we neglect the single step that lies in front of our feet. So we need the wisdom of God to guide us in both matters, and the divine word does not fail us. The promise of 1 Samuel 2:9 says, "He will guard the feet of his faithful ones." But Paul lifted his eyes to his ultimate goal and remarked, "I press on toward the goal" (Philippians 3:14). The ultimate goal informed his daily effort, and his daily effort pointed unerringly toward his ultimate goal.

And it is God's good intention to illuminate both the step we take today and the final destiny that gives meaning to our daily steps.

In this stanza, named *Sameka*–the fifteenth letter of the Hebrew alphabet–the first word, which begins with that letter, is translated "double-minded." The word occurs only here and twice in the epistle of James. But though the word is rare, the tragic condition it describes is common, as it was when Psalm 119 was written. It refers to one who is not fully convinced and tries to "carry water on both shoulders," as the saying puts it.

Elijah, offended by the "double-mindedness" of the people of his day, confronted the people on Mount Carmel, challenging them, "How long will you go limping with two different opinions? If the LORD is God, follow him. But if Baal, then follow him" (1 Kings 18:21).

Jesus also found double-mindedness distasteful and warned the people who heard his Sermon on the Mount, "No one can serve two masters; for a slave will either hate the one and love the other, or be devoted to the one and despise the other. You cannot serve God and wealth" (Matthew 6:24).

Indeed, so repugnant was this half-hearted religion that the risen Christ condemned it in his letter to the church at Laodicea, "I know your works; you are neither cold nor hot. So, because you are lukewarm, and neither cold nor hot, I am about to spit you out of my mouth" (Revelation 3:15–16).

A minister once noticed that whenever he mentioned the name of the devil from the pulpit, a woman in his congregation bowed her head, as though in reverence. He asked her once about this curious custom, and she replied, "Well, my dear, courtesy costs nothing, and one never knows where one might find oneself."

But such "courtesy" costs a great deal indeed. It robs us of the glorious treasures of faith that are available only to those who give their hearts to God without reservation.

Surely we have learned from sad experience that we don't always get what we pay for, but we always pay for what we get. And a religion that costs us nothing, gives us nothing. God will not reside in a heart that also makes room for lesser gods or smaller goals.

DAY 134
Read Psalm 119:121–128

There is both impudence and impatience in the petulant demand, "It is time for the LORD to act, for your law has been broken" (v. 126). So the psalmist scolds the Lord, trying to hold those heavenly feet to the fires of human logic. You promised, Lord, to be on the side of your faithful ones and to punish those who disobey your commands. Now look at you!–hiding your apathy behind the clouds of mystery. Don't just stand there; do something!

When we are very young and first begin to learn about prayer, we think of prayer in the same way we think of a letter to Santa Claus, and we send up a list of wishes to God, and if we are very good little boys and girls, maybe God will climb down our chimney and give us what we asked for. Or we see prayer as a kind of heavenly vending machine, in which we put a nickel's worth of prayer and get out a nickel's worth of answer.

But early failures and disappointments lead us to suspect that instead of being like a spiritual vending machine, prayer is more like a spiritual slot machine, with several elements involved: how we pray, what kind of faith we have, how persistent we are, whether what we want is God's will, and so on. And only when all those many elements fall accurately into place do we hit the jackpot. And only the very persistent in prayer–like the die-hard players of the one-armed bandits in Las Vegas–ever beat the odds and get any sweepstakes answers to prayer. And then there is always the suspicion that it was all a matter of luck anyway, and the same results could probably have been obtained without prayer.

Prayer is not a way to get God to act, but a way to bring ourselves into the sphere of grace, in which we allow the benevolent power of God to transform our understandings and desires and in which God can give us the gifts of grace that will augment what we are, to make us able to do what God asks.

Understood in this way, our prayers are always answered, and God always acts, in the way and at the time God knows is best for us.

Who of us has not had the experience of studying the road map of an unfamiliar locale and making no sense of the squiggly red, blue, and black lines and the strange names and symbols? Then comes the dawning realization that the last flap of the map has not been unfolded. And when that last portion of the map is unfolded, all the lines and symbols begin to make sense, and you see where it all leads.

All life conforms to that paradigm. We cannot understand all of the past, or the present, or the future. Strange events and circumstances confront us, and we can make no sense of life. But there is a discipline of delayed revelation, and we know that as life unfolds, we will see more and understand more. And when the last flap is unfolded, everything will be clear.

One of the most useful tools in our quest to understand life is the Bible. But even the Holy Scriptures do not open their full truth to us at first glance. Rather, as the psalmist says, "The unfolding of your words gives light" (v. 130). The Hebrew word for "unfolding" is used elsewhere in the Bible to describe the opening of the doors of the temple (2 Chronicles 29:3). As the unfolding of a road map gives us gradually increasing understanding, and as the opening of the doors of the temple invites us to discover the presence of God, so the study of the scriptures gives us light for life's journey and opportunity for companionship with God.

Because the Bible is a holy instrument, God often speaks through it, in strange, unexpected ways, to give you the light you need for shining on today's path.

A man who had undergone severe troubles through a long period of suffering finally turned to the Bible in an attempt to find something to help him understand and cope with his circumstances. He happened to open the Bible to the second chapter of Luke, where he read the *King James Version*'s familiar words "It came to pass." And he stopped at that point, having learned the strange but undeniable truth that everything that happens to us is transient and evanescent. All our pains and problems are "here today and gone tomorrow." But in the midst of all this fleeting misfortune is the unchanging God, whose love for us is as constant as the stars.

Keep unfolding the word of God. Perhaps the very next flap you unfold will speak to you the truth you need most to hear.

"Your promise is well tried," the psalmist says here in verse 140, "and your servant loves it." Like the hamburger fast-food chain that boasts "ten billion served," there is a certain confidence to be gained in the realization that uncountable millions of people have tried God's promise and have found it trustworthy. What, precisely, has the Lord promised us that we can depend on?

First, God has promised to be with us always, no matter what circumstances may confront us. "And remember, I am with you always, to the end of the age," Jesus assured his disciples in his last spoken word (Matthew 28:20). God did not promise to protect you from all danger, but you have God's word that there will be a holy presence with you, guiding your steps and providing a safe passage through the storms.

God has not promised that your shoulders will never have to bear heavy burdens, but God did promise that you will never be tested beyond your endurance. "God is faithful, and...will not let you be tested beyond your strength, but with the testing...will also provide the way out so that you may be able to endure it" (1 Corinthians 10:13). The same God that created the burden on your shoulders made the shoulders that carry the burden, and God assures us that they will be a matched set.

God has not promised that we will never succumb to evil, but God has assured us that no sin is so grievous and no guilt so egregious that it can block our return to God. "Him who comes to me I will not cast out," Jesus promised (John 6:37, RSV). No ifs, ands, or buts, no footnotes claiming exceptions. "I will not cast out." Period.

God has not promised that our every battle will be victorious– only our last one. He who looked like the world's most miserable ninety-pound weakling on Friday afternoon on a hill just outside Jerusalem became the all-time champion weight lifter on Sunday, lifting the stone that sealed his tomb, and lifting the death sentence from all our souls. He gave the world its most poignant proof of the truth of the saying, "Weeping may linger for the night, but joy comes with the morning" (Psalm 30:5).

God has not promised that everything that comes to you will be good, but that in all things, God will work for your good if you love God and are called according to God's purpose.

What more could anyone ask?

DAY 137
Read Psalm 119:145–152

There is a word in this psalm that provides a rationale for keeping the language of the Bible close to the vernacular of the day. In the 147th verse we read (in the *King James Version*), "I prevented the dawning of the morning." In 1611 C.E., when the *King James Version* was published, the word *prevent* meant "to come before." In the nearly four centuries since that time, that word has come to mean "prohibit" or "keep from happening." So the verse really means, "I come before the dawn," or, as the *New Revised Standard Version* puts it, "I rise before dawn."

Even though the older translation has been updated, it suggests a lesson that ought to be taken seriously. No one can "prevent" the dawn. The daily miracle of sunrise is so dependable that even the atomic clocks in observatories can be tested for accuracy by comparing them with the arrival of dawn. And the precise moment of "dawn's early light" may be confidently predicted for centuries in advance. You cannot hold back the dawn.

And although no one in his right mind would attempt to alter so mathematically dependable a schedule, there are those people who continue to oppose the coming of light in other ways.

An old saying reminds us "there is nothing so powerful as an idea whose time has come." But the arrival of the light of a new day in race relations was opposed by many people, who went to extraordinary lengths to try to hold back that dawn. Every scientific advance has been challenged by those who preferred the dark night of ignorance to the dawning of new light.

When Christ's new kingdom was struggling for birth, the established religion of the day felt itself threatened by the new and authorized persecution and martyrdom as tools to try to keep that sunrise from lighting up the world. But a wise leader named Gamaliel warned his colleagues, "If this plan or this undertaking is of human origin, it will fail; but if it is of God, you will not be able to overthrow [it]…You may even be found fighting against God" (Acts 5:38–39).

Beware of attempting to prevent the sunrise of any new day. Indeed, you may want to "rise before dawn" to pray to God that you may always be found on the side of God's truth, even when that truth wears new clothes.

DAY 138
Read Psalm 119:153–160

The familiar passage in Shakespeare's *Hamlet* quotes Lord Polonius as saying to Laertes:

> To thine own self be true,
> And it must follow, as the night the day,
> Thou canst not then be false to any man.

The psalmist, in this stanza, is making the same appeal to God's honor: Just be yourself, Lord, and I will trust the result.

Three times the psalmist begs for his life (twice he says "give me life" [vv. 154, 156] and once "preserve my life" [v. 159]). Each time he bases his request on God's honor: "according to your promise" (v. 154), or "according to your justice" (v. 156), or "according to your steadfast love" (v. 159). Just be your affirming, merciful, loving self, Lord. Do not give me what I deserve, but what your own character demands.

In this understanding the psalmist reveals a perception of God that was not to be commonly accepted until Christ made it clear in his life and teachings: God's dealings with us are not predicated on what we are, but on what God is.

In Jesus' classic story of the prodigal son, the father's magnanimous welcome and restoration of the wayward youth was due, in no respect at all, to what the prodigal was or had done, but in every respect to what the father was. That gracious parent was being true to himself. He could not, then, be false to anyone.

Even after all these centuries of marveling at this magnificent fact, we still find it difficult to wrap our minds around such a noble concept. We keep thinking that we must do something to earn what we ask of God. But we could never earn or deserve God's matchless grace. All we can do is accept it, humbly and gratefully, and live a life that reflects that gratitude.

Unfortunately, we often fail to read the last chapter of the story of the prodigal, in which we see the tragedy of one who insists on computing his worth on the grounds of his own effort. The elder brother demanded justice because he had earned it by his laborious effort. But when we insist on setting the scales of our own justice, we will be condemned to accept the result.

DAY 139
Read Psalm 119:161–168

"Great peace have those who love your law," the psalmist says (v. 165). *Shalom* is the Hebrew word used here. It refers not to an absence of conflict, but to a certain calm of soul that provides a shelter of confidence and joy, even when the battle is in full sway. It is the tranquility that feels the grip of God's hand on our shoulder, even when chaos has erupted around us. It is the knowledge that sometimes the Lord calms the storm, but at other times the Lord lets the storm rage and calms the child. It is the certainty that although we may not know what the future holds, we know who holds the future.

Isaiah's great promise is, "Those of steadfast mind you keep in peace—in peace because they trust in you" (Isaiah 26:3).

What would you do if you became aware of the fact that you had less than twenty-four hours to live? Probably most of us would be so anxious and troubled that we would go to pieces and be so emotionally paralyzed that we would not be able to do anything productive. But think of this man who made that shocking discovery: less than twenty-four hours to live! And yet he went calmly about his work, approaching each encounter with patience and compassion and fulfilling his assigned tasks competently and calmly. Even when those hours dwindled to minutes, he was still able to react to people with sensitivity and concern. At the very last he revealed the secret of his peace: "Father," he prayed, "into thy hands I commit my spirit" (Luke 23:46, RSV).

"Oh," we say in disappointment, "you mean Jesus. That's different." But the whole point of it is that it wasn't any different. Jesus was young, in good health, doing the most important work ever attempted, and had every bit as much reason to want to go on living as you do. But he was able to enjoy a certain peace because he had put what was dearest to him—his very life—into hands that were loving and strong, capable of dealing with any disaster.

The word we translate "commit" was, in the original Greek, *paratheke,* which is usually translated "deposit." He knew, as he faced the cross, that he was not giving his life away or throwing it away. He had invested it where he knew it was safe, and from where he could withdraw it again. That was the secret of his *shalom.*

And if your mind is centered on God, and your heart is fixed on God, you will enjoy a peace that passes all understanding.

At the very end of this prodigious psalm, the writer confesses that he is like a lost sheep, having somehow, despite all his noble intentions to the contrary, missed the goal of faithfulness he had set for his own life. In this self-revelation we can find a mirror image of our own earnest but often faulty pilgrimage. With the apostle Paul we can confess, "I do not understand my own actions. For I do not do what I want, but I do the very thing I hate" (Romans 7:15). Even our attempts at correcting our course are often poorly conceived or only partially fulfilled.

So what is the honest psalmist to do? Is he to turn over a new leaf and close his eyes tightly and repeat, like a mantra, the formula of *The Little Engine That Could,* "I think I can, I think I can, I think I can"? No, it is clear that the psalmist had discovered–as we have–the limitations of such efforts at self-empowerment. We can no longer trust our efforts to find God's presence and wring from God's promises the help we need. God is not a prize to be won by our initiative.

But in a splendidly humble surrender to his own failure and a glorious understanding of God's never-ending concern for us, the psalmist offers himself to be found by the seeking God: "Seek out your servant" (v. 176).

We often speak of "seeking God" or "finding God," as though God intentionally hides from our search, until we have stumbled on the proper combination for pinning down the Holy Spirit. Rather, we ought to think of ourselves not as the seekers but as the sought.

Jesus made it clear to Zacchaeus: "The Son of Man came to seek and to save the lost" (Luke 19:9). God is the seeker; we are the sought. And only when we give up hiding from God and allow ourselves to be brought into God's sheltering arms will we know the joy of belonging to the Eternal God.

Jacob learned it at the ford of the Jabbok. After a long night of striving, seeking, pursuing, and attempting to "tame" God, he surrendered, and he allowed himself to be found by God and given a new name and a new understanding. We do not "win" in this confrontation with God unless we are willing to lose. We will never "find" God until we allow ourselves to be found by God.

And when we do that, the shepherd carries us home on his shoulder, shouting with delight, "Rejoice with me, for I have found the lost."

Psalms 120 through 134 are all identified as "songs of ascent." It is believed that these songs were specifically written and used by pilgrims as they traveled toward Jerusalem. Any trip to Jerusalem from anywhere else would be an arduous climb, inasmuch as Jerusalem was situated on the crest of the mountainous spine that runs from the north of Israel to its south. In all probability these songs were sung by pilgrims to elevate their spirits while the ascent was taking its toll on their bodies.

There is an ancient Jewish tradition that these fifteen "songs of ascent" were sung to accompany the act of climbing the fifteen steps that led from the court of the women, in the temple, to the court of the men. Although the tradition invites certain interesting comments, it is unlikely that the legend was based in fact.

What is more certain is that these—and all the other—Psalms were collected and put into their present form after the fall of Jerusalem in 70 C.E. From that day until 1948, when the United Nations partitioned Palestine to create a homeland for Jewish people, those of Hebrew descent had no homeland. They lived as sojourners, or as "strangers in a strange land." These songs of pilgrimage were in frequent use by these people, who wondered, in despair, "How could we sing the LORD's song in a foreign land?" (Psalm 137:4).

The fact is that people of faith have always had to live in a foreign and often hostile environment. The word *parish,* by which we refer to a Christian congregation, is derived from the Greek word *paroichia,* which means a body of aliens living together in a foreign land.

The author of the Hebrew epistle lauded the heroes of the faith and said of them, "All of these died in faith without having received the promises, but from a distance they saw and greeted them. They confessed that they were strangers and foreigners on the earth" (Hebrews 11:13).

But we are also sojourners—travelers. The Christian life is a journey, and however long a journey may be, it must be traveled one day at a time. Think of the elderly woman who reported the testimony in her Bible study group: "I ain't what I ought to be, and I ain't what I'm going to be. But thank the Lord, I ain't what I used to be, and I'm marchin'!"

That's a song of ascent!

DAY 142
Read Psalm 121

There is always a certain degree of anxiety connected with departing on a journey. Will your loved ones, staying at home, remain well during your absence? Will your home remain safe from marauders? Will your strength and resources be sufficient to complete the journey?

If today's traveler feels those anxieties, with air-conditioned comfort in an automobile and with credit cards to guarantee against unexpected misfortunes, imagine the apprehension felt by pilgrims in Old Testament times! What security could they feel in their journey along rocky paths with wild animals and highwaymen and a thousand other perils to threaten them?

One can almost feel the sense of relief when, at last, they could look toward the western horizon and see Mount Zion and, shining like a welcoming beacon, the holy temple. How that vista must have quickened their steps and recharged their strength! It was as if the Lord were standing on that mountaintop, inviting the pilgrim and promising the assurance of security and satisfaction.

"He who keeps Israel will neither slumber nor sleep" (v. 4). The unblinking eye of divine compassion will watch over the flock of the Lord's people. If God, who created the heavens and the earth and maintains the universe with meticulous care, provides for each lily of the field and every sparrow in the air, how much more will that divine concern wrap every person with protective care.

In London, during the nightly bombardment from Nazi rockets, one elderly woman seemed completely unconcerned about her personal safety. She claimed to be able to sleep peacefully every night. Someone asked her how she could sleep so soundly, when bombs were exploding all around her neighborhood. She replied, "I read that the Lord neither slumbers nor sleeps, so I figure, what's the use of the both of us staying awake?"

And we have the promise that the Lord is at both ends of our journey. God was with us when it began, and God will be at the end of our journey, inviting us into heaven's holy presence.

And this promise embraces not only the perilous present, but all the time to come, "from this time on and forevermore" (v. 8).

What pilgrim would not find comfort in such assurances?

Daily life in Israel was a grim affair in Old Testament times. There was little to relieve the struggle for food and the quest for a measure of security against the harsh realities of life. But like oases of celebration dotting the forbidding landscape of the desert were the festivals that drew Hebrew people to the major city of Jerusalem. Deuteronomy 16:16 lists three feasts at which attendance in Jerusalem was obligatory for all adult males: Passover (or the Feast of Unleavened Bread) in the spring; Pentecost (or the Feast of Weeks), coming fifty days after Passover; and Succoth (or the Feast of Tabernacles) in the autumn.

At the core of these celebrations were a religious commemoration of God's mercy to Israel in the past and thanksgiving for the annual bounty of nature's goodness. But equally important were the subsidiary diversions of homecoming, visiting with old friends and family members, singing the "old songs," and enjoying the rare phenomenon of plenty of good food to eat.

Because each festival was also a time when the whole nation of Israel could be said to have gathered together, certain political functions were also fulfilled at these occasions. Civil courts were set up to settle small disputes ("the thrones for judgment were set up" [v. 5]).

Little wonder the people were "glad" when invited to "go to the house of the LORD" (v. 1). To these people, the "house of the Lord" was not the local synagogue, but the city of Jerusalem and the temple that gave the city its prominence.

But the mood of gladness is one that is deserved by a visit to any house of God. Unfortunately, too many churches permit services that are arid, joyless, and eminently forgettable.

A cartoon in the *New Yorker* magazine depicted a clergyman being carried out the doors of a church by a mob of happy people who were smiling, laughing, and throwing confetti into the air. An observer, indicating the fortunate pastor, asked his companion, "What on earth do you suppose he preached about?" Whatever it was, the church needs to learn it and proclaim it from the pulpit. The gospel is, first and best of all, good news. And hearing it told in a manner that fits the subject should make anyone glad.

DAY 144
Read Psalm 123

The people of Israel enjoyed a splendid sense of their own identity. They believed themselves to be God's very special people and, as such, drew their self-image from the supremacy of their senior partner. As their God was above all other gods, so they—God's people—were a notch or two above all other people. It was especially humiliating to them, therefore, when they were forced to submit to the governance of pagans.

Many scholars believe this psalm came out of the time of Israel's Babylonian captivity. Through the Old Testament stories of Daniel and Shadrach, Meshach, and Abednego, we see clearly how the Babylonians sought to humiliate the Hebrew people into submission and how stubbornly the Hebrews refused to comply.

So in this psalm the people pour out their complaint and prayer: "Have mercy upon us, O LORD...for we have had more than enough of contempt" (v. 3).

A young man, swept along in the "partying" mood of his fraternity, was with his brothers at a bar where alcohol flowed freely and various other degrading opportunities were present in abundance. But the young man, who cherished his Christian faith and life, finally drew back from the abyss of corruption at the last moment. As he left the bar, he was heard to say, "I am better than this!"

Are you better than what your activities and attitudes and allegiances would say about you? As a child of God, you ought to reach higher in your character aspirations than other people. And you should not be intimidated by those who abide by a lower standard than you do. They have their destiny in their own hands. But you have your destiny in your hands. Don't give something so precious to those who don't understand how, as a child of God, you are a very special person.

Many parents of adolescents have adopted the custom of reminding their sons or daughters as they leave the house for an evening's entertainment, "Remember who you are!" You can bear the contempt others show toward you as long as you do not hold yourself in contempt.

Is God on our side? When a nation goes to war against another, it is not uncommon to hear both sides claiming that "God is on our side." Napoleon is reported to have said to the pope, who made that claim, that "God is on the side of the army that has the most battalions." But despite that cynical view, it must be understood that God is always on the side of God. And any nation or individual that seeks to conform to or to accomplish the will of God can expect the Lord to provide the extra strength and endurance that result from compliance with God's ultimate purpose.

Imagine a fantasy in which two opposing armies have gathered at the seashore at low tide. One army is armed with weapons and conveyances that are meant for conflict on dry land. The other army, believing that high tide will surely follow low tide, has equipped itself with boats and equipment meant for conflict in the water. Surely the latter army will discover, when the tide comes in, the forces of nature cooperating with their efforts, and may later claim that God was on their side, guaranteeing their victory. God will always honor those who seek to understand and cooperate with God's laws.

In our belief in God and our obedience to God's laws, we put ourselves in a position in which the energies of God can be harnessed. We may expect the laws that we respect will respect us.

The apostle Paul celebrated this reliance on God's will in his triumphant words, "If God is for us, who is against us?" (Romans 8:31). Martin Luther's majestic hymn, "A Mighty Fortress Is Our God," includes these lines:

> Did we in our own strength confide, our striving would be losing,
> but there is one who takes our side, the one of God's own choosing.

And in a later stanza:

> We will not fear, for God has willed His truth to triumph through us.
> (Martin Luther, translated by Frederick Hedge, adapted by Ruth Duck)

It is God's truth that will triumph. And if we are on the side of God's truth, then we have placed ourselves on the side that God must favor and that will ultimately succeed.

Because this psalm is another in a series of psalms of ascent, we may well understand that it was recited (or sung) by pilgrims on their way to Jerusalem. What a great joy must have been experienced by those weary travelers when at last they could see, on the horizon, the broken skyline of the Holy City, surrounded by mountains. The vista gave them a visual parable: As the city was surrounded (and protected from enemies) by mountains, so God was always present, encircling them with loving favor and safeguarding them from their enemies. The psalm reflects the picture painted in an earlier psalm of ascent: "I lift up my eyes to the hills—from where will my help come? My help comes from the LORD" (Psalm 121:1–2).

The sight of mountains evokes from the soul a largeness of spirit and an appreciation for the divine hand that framed them. Poet Olive Tilford Dargan, in her poem "Twilight," said:

The mountains lie in curves so tender
I want to lay my arm about them
As God does.

An old story, almost lost to the memory, depicts a boy named Ernest who grew up in the shadow of a mountain, on whose rocky side the face of a man seemed visible. That "Great Stone Face" drew his attention every day and in almost every hour of the day. When he grew up, neighbors and friends recognized that the lad's countenance had assumed the features of that rocky visage. He had become what he admired.

And so do we all. Those whose daily sights are lifted up by mountains around them assume a certain greatness of heart and elevation of attention. And those who daily seek the presence of God assume those qualities of character and personality that belong to God.

After spending forty days on Mount Sinai, seeking from God the word that became the Ten Commandments, Moses returned to the plain where the people of Israel had encamped. And Moses' face glowed so brilliantly, as a result of his companionship with God, that the people could not look at him (Exodus 34:33–35).

Does the radiance of God's presence light up your face when you have spent time in the presence of the Holy? Does anyone say to you, as Jacob said to his forgiving brother, Esau, "To see your face is like seeing the face of God"? (Genesis 33:10).

DAY 147
Read Psalm 126

One of Edna St. Vincent Millay's sonnets depicts a farmer whose land has been inundated by a flood. Everything he owns is now under water. It is evening as he rows away from the scene of the disaster in a little rowboat. His heart grieves for the immensity of his loss. But the picture has a hint of hope in it, for, as the concluding line says, he rows away "with twisted face, and pocket full of seeds."

That picture is reminiscent of Psalm 126, which closes with words that have become familiar to us because of the hymn tune to which they were set: "He that goes forth weeping, bearing the seed for sowing, shall come home with shouts of joy, bringing his sheaves with him" (v. 6, RSV).

The psalmist was writing in a time "between the times" of Hebrew history. Behind them were the glorious days of God's visible leadership and abundant blessing. Gone were the times when righteousness had exalted their nation. But now, in the moment of its writing, the psalm reflects an impotent and inglorious present. The people's faithlessness had made them vulnerable to the attack of foreign invaders and their bondage to pagans. What circumstance could be more detested than the abomination of the present?

But their faith looked up to a future filled with hope. "Restore our fortunes," they prayed to God, "like the watercourses in the Negeb" (v. 4). The Negeb was the desert south of Israel. Perhaps there was a time when streams in the desert made that inhospitable place blossom like a rose, but not now! But God could once again bring water to the desolated plain, and springtime of new life would be possible.

And the secret of that future was the hope that remained in the hearts of the people. Where hope remains alive, there are seeds for tomorrow's harvest.

A retired minister relishes the memory of a woman in his first pastorate who was fast approaching her ninetieth birthday. Although the weight of her years had bowed her legs and a childhood case of smallpox made her eyes appear to be looking in opposite directions, she was stubbornly young at heart. One day the minister went to call on her and found her in the backyard planting an apple tree. He asked, "Do you expect to eat apples from this tree?" "Someone will," she replied. And it was that hope, that "pocket full of seeds," that kept her looking forward.

DAY 148
Read Psalm 127

Bible scholar James Limburg remembers the day an associate said to him, "I just had one of those nights when I was lying awake, baby-sitting the world." Although many of us qualify as those who try, at times, to "baby-sit" the whole world, we realize that such an effort is useless, because God never takes hands off this world. God made it; God loves it; God protects and provides for it. And in those divine functions, God doesn't need our help.

In two vivid metaphors the psalmist reminds us of God's care and the futility of all human attempts to provide the protection that only God can give. "Unless the LORD builds the house, those who build it labor in vain. Unless the LORD guards the city, the guard keeps watch in vain" (v. 1).

Twenty-first-century parents are generally overachievers in matters of providing for the health of their children. They are careful to see to the dental, optical, and physical needs of their offspring. And the children's social graces are not neglected. They are given music lessons, dancing lessons, and instructions in etiquette. The children are dressed in the latest juvenile fashions. They are expert in the use of computers and other electronic gadgets. They are enrolled in team sports and are appropriately uniformed. But sadly, in too many cases, these healthy, intelligent, refined young paragons have souls that are starved and neglected.

When Moses was negotiating with Pharaoh for the release of the Hebrew slaves, Pharaoh offered several compromises. In one of them the Egyptian potentate suggested that Moses and the other adults could leave Egypt if they would let their children stay behind. Pharaoh surely reasoned that the adults would be gone soon enough anyway, but as long as they stayed in control of the children, they were in control of the future. But Moses was adamant in his reply: "We will go with our young and our old; we will go with our sons and daughters" (Exodus 10:9). But too many nominal Christian parents have left their children behind in Egypt,

Unless the Lord builds the house—and the home—no parental controls or cautions will protect the children against the ultimate penalties of growing up pagan.

DAY 149
Read Psalm 128

This psalm of "traditional family values" is one that might be the subject of a sampler to be hung on the walls of a home. It extols the importance of work and its rewards and sees the faithfulness of a good wife as a divine blessing and the production of children as a virtue. Even grandchildren are trotted out to be enumerated as blessings from God. Finally, the nation at peace completes the picture of the joys and rewards of faithfulness to God and God's law.

But as tranquil and blissful a picture as that presented in the psalm, one cannot help but overhear the complaints of those who have, through no fault of their own, been denied such evidences of divine favor. What about the people who cannot work, who would love to know the satisfaction of purposeful labor, but cannot, either because of their health or age or an economy in which many people simply are shut out of the workforce?

And what comfort can be offered those for whom marriage is not an option. "One man for every woman; one woman for every man" is hardly a pattern that can be applied in a culture in which there is a chronic imbalance in the general population and in which marriage not a relationship of choice for many.

And surely we have, as a society, outgrown the notion that the production of children is the destiny to be desired by all people. Whereas previous cultures may have looked with disfavor on women who remained "barren," our overpopulated world should no longer urge the genesis of children as the only function of marriage.

And even grandchildren, as cherished as they are, cannot be seen as the ultimate blessing that demonstrates God's reward for the longevity of a marriage relationship.

And although one's nation at peace is a bounty greatly to be desired, one cannot look on its absence as God's penalty to the individuals in that nation, who may, themselves, be people of peace.

Nevertheless, most of us have a right to relish the ability and the opportunity to work, the joys of family life in a harmonious home, the joys brought to us by our children and grandchildren, and the privilege of living in a nation at peace.

And in a world that tends to put a price tag on everything, it is heartening to be reminded, by this list of superlative assets, that the best things in life are free.

DAY 150
Read Psalm 129

After capturing Washington, D.C., and burning several public buildings (including the White House), the British forces headed for Baltimore. On the morning of September 13, 1814, British bomb ships began hurling shells toward Fort McHenry. The bombardment continued through the rainy night, and citizens of the new republic began to fear that in this war, begun in 1812, their country would lose its independence.

Anxiously awaiting news of the battle's outcome, Francis Scott Key utilized the first light of the new dawn to train his telescope to Fort McHenry. He was cheered by the sight of the American flag, still waving in the morning breeze, over the scene of the devastation. The war was not over, but the sight of that flag, raised in defiance against the invaders, provided evidence that the nation was still free and the tide of battle had turned in their favor.

In a song he wrote on that occasion, he spoke of that flag, saying that the light from the gunfire "gave proof through the night that our flag was still there." The war was not over, but his faith was renewed and his hope restored by that ensign.

So the people of Israel had suffered many attacks from their enemies. Their history was red with the blood of martyrs. But their indomitable spirit found their faith renewed and their hope restored whenever their trust in God broke through the storms to give them proof that God was still there, still watching over the flock, still leading them to ultimate victory.

Hope is one of the most stubborn graces God presses upon us. God pressed it upon Noah in the form of one olive leaf in the beak of a dove. Skeptics might have scoffed at that as a meaningless accident, an irrelevant coincidence, a ridiculous tokenism, a freakish nothing; but with the world around him brought to a standstill by a monstrously comprehensive flood, Noah could ill afford such petulance. One olive leaf was all there was, and had he discounted that, he might never have dared to leave the ark and begin again. He would have perished there in fear and despair and bitterness.

But there is always an olive leaf, isn't there? There is always a flag waving above the battlefield, always a tiny hint from a God who refuses to stay dead, that a new tomorrow is coming for those who have enough outrageous faith to believe in the God who hides such tokens of hope in the sands of life.

This psalm is traditionally known as *De Profundis,* which is the Latin translation of its first words, "Out of the depths." Although the exact nature of the extremity thus described is not known, we can all identify with the feeling suggested.

Sometimes the depression is a result of our own guilty conscience. We have sinned, and the memory of that shoddy deed tarnishes our peace of mind. Clearly the dejection felt by the psalmist was linked to guilt, for the Psalm also begs God's forgiveness and redemption. And as long as God remembers our sin, we have no right to forget it. But when God forgives our sin, we have no right to remember it. It is no longer ours.

But it doesn't make much difference, when we are hurting, whether we brought it on ourselves or not. Innocent or guilty, when we are in the depths, we hurt. Sometimes we are entirely blameless, but that doesn't make us feel any better, though such a discovery ought to stir the consciences of those who permit unjust circumstances to continue to make victims of innocent people.

And of course there are times when we are the victims of the cruelty of other people. Even Jesus could not escape the merciless barbarity of those who felt no allegiance to the reign of love and kindness that refined Jesus' actions.

But there is wisdom in the reply of a man who had fallen into a pit, and who was offered pity from a passerby who asked, "How did you get in there?" The victim replied, "How I got in here is not the point, since I don't intend to do it again. The thing that interests me is, how do I get out of here?" And that's what we need to know.

An amusing story is told of an old mule that had outlived his usefulness. The owner sought to dispose of the mule by throwing him down a well. But the mule survived the trip and brayed reproachfully when the owner looked down and saw the animal's sad eyes looking up at him. Clearly something more had to be done. So the owner dumped load after load of dirt into the well to bury the mule. But the mule calmly climbed up on each load of dirt when it descended upon him and, when the dirt reached the top, serenely walked away.

You may not be able to do everything to extricate yourself from the depths, but *you can do something!* And little by little, by pulling yourself above the daily ration of dirt that descends upon you, you will eventually find yourself "out of the depths."

A woman who had taken numerous courses in first aid came, one day, upon the scene of an accident. As she recalled the occasion later, she said, "When I saw all that human misery and injury, I realized that here was the opportunity to put my first aid training to good use. So I sat right down, put my head between my knees, and *I didn't faint!*"

As short-sighted and self-centered as that attitude might appear, sometimes the best our faith can do is to keep us from falling victim to the circumstances we face. Because this is a psalm of David, we can assume that the psalmist had experienced numerous occasions when his faith emboldened him to heroic and sacrificial endeavors. This was the same David who wrote, "Though an army encamp against me, my heart shall not fear" (Psalm 27:3) and "Contend, O LORD, with those who contend with me" (Psalm 35:1). He knew the Lord as his ally in battle and as his shield and armor.

But there were also those times when David's faith was sorely tested, not by danger, but by the more subtle enemy of despair. In such times, David experienced the rescue of his soul through the simple blessing of survival. Numerous aphorisms teach us the common sense of doing the best we can in unfortunate circumstances, when a thrilling victory is not a realistic expectation. "If life hands you lemons, make lemonade," is one. Here is another: "When you come to the end of your rope, tie a knot and hang on."

But there come those times when even such minor victories are beyond our reach. At such times, we can receive from the Lord the comfort that a baby knows when nursing at the mother's breast. We may not have the key to unlock the perplexities we face, or the courage to launch an offensive against them, but at the very least we can accept—gratefully and humbly—the comfort and peace a loving God gladly gives to a frightened child. And there are times when that is quite enough.

For centuries beyond the reach of memory, Jewish people have cherished the concept of their being a chosen people. Scripture justifies their claim. In Psalm 33 we read, "Happy is the nation whose God is the LORD, the people whom he has chosen as a heritage" (Psalm 33:12). And in Psalm 132 there is "For the LORD has chosen Zion; he has desired it for his habitation" (v. 13).

So God chose both the people and the place of their habitation. But why? It was not for special privilege, but for special responsibility. It was an ancient dream, first given to Abraham, who left his homeland of Ur in the Chaldees and went out "not knowing where he was going" (Hebrews 11:8), always chasing the magnificent but always just-out-of-reach vision of ethereal glory in a specific and earthly time and place.

The dream came close to fulfillment under the leadership of David but dissolved in the tears of David's egregious proof of his sinful nature. And when the glorious temple seemed to merit the conclusion that God's kingdom had come on earth, and in that special city, Solomon provided the same sort of evidence that his father, David, had given, that human hands were unreliable vessels for creating a resting place for the Holy God.

Unfortunately, when one came whose divine credentials brought to earth humankind's greatest hope for realizing the kingdom of heaven, people were looking for a different kind of kingdom.

God still chooses persons for special responsibility and chooses places for holy habitation. But God chooses every human heart to be the divine choice. We confirm and activate that choice by the endorsement of our willingness to be what and where God wants us to be.

A kindergarten teacher sent permission slips home for all the children's parents to sign, indicating that, if chosen by lot, they would have the privilege of taking care of the class's pet hamster during the summer months. When the couple chosen for the honor asked how they could have been so fortunate, the teacher replied, "Because you were the only ones who signed the permission slip."

Who are God's chosen people today? Whoever signs the permission slip, allowing God to inhabit our hearts.

Tradition claims that when there were still only two automobiles in the entire metropolis of Kansas City, Missouri, those two vehicles collided at the busy intersection of Walnut and Main Streets. It was a vivid enactment of one of earth's earliest tragedies: When there were just two brothers in all the world (Cain and Abel), one rose up in anger and slew the other. How God must have grieved for that rupture in the family bond! And how God must grieve every bitter fruit of that incident that fragments the human family today.

It is obviously the divine intention that all God's children should regard themselves as brothers and sisters to one another. And any breach of that family relationship is an offense against God.

To be sure, the human family has become quite large, and the differences that separate us into factions have become both exceedingly numerous and difficult to overlook. But if we are sisters and brothers to one another, that one fact should make it possible for us to live together in unity.

The ancient Greek philosopher Epictetus originated the principle of the two handles. He said, in effect, that everything in life has two handles. By one handle you can carry it; by the other you cannot. Epictetus gave an example to explain what he meant. He said, "If your brother offends you, you cannot carry the relationship by the handle of the offense. If you brood over the offense, the estrangement between you and your brother will only grow more and more bitter. But you can carry it by reminding yourself that the man is your brother. Carry the estrangement by the handle of your brotherhood, and you will have some hope of reconciliation."

How sad and how bitter it is when brothers and sisters are alienated. But how good and pleasant it is when those kinsfolk find a common denominator that makes them realize their family relationship.

As God once said through Joseph to his brothers in Egypt, so God says to us: "You shall not see my face, unless your brother is with you" (Genesis 43:5).

From early childhood many of us learned to pray "Now I lay me down to sleep; I pray the Lord my soul to keep." Perhaps from that early training, we have come to see a mystic connection between the nighttime and prayer. All day long our minds are occupied with the busyness of the chores to be done and dangers to be faced. There is little time for the soul to relax and find comfort in the presence of God. But when the clamor and the demands diminish and our bodies find repose, our spirits trace their origin to the Great Spirit from which they were given birth. Although God is not nearer to us in the dark, at least we are nearer to God.

With no one to see or hear us but God, we come to a greater realization of who we are and whose we are. Often such a realization convicts us of the guilt of our daytime mistakes and failures, and we seek the healing that God's forgiveness provides. And as sleep "knits up the raveled sleeve of care," and our bodies are renewed by the restorative powers of sleep, so our souls often find renewal in the Godward thoughts and meditations that attend our stillness.

But the quietness of the night should also spur us to a remembrance of the many who are on duty at night—the hospital personnel, the police and fire departments, the security guards, and others whose alertness at night makes it possible for us to know a measure of peace.

In the temple there were special attendants whose prayers through the nighttime hours perpetuated the relationship between God and the people. These "third-watch worshipers" assured the people that there was never a time when someone was not standing at their post, maintaining the relationship between the Shepherd and the flock.

This psalm pays tribute to those "who stand by night in the house of the Lord" (v. 1).

We have no idea how those people were selected for their special nighttime duty. Perhaps they volunteered for their special responsibility. One must ask: Is anyone praying now, in those long night hours, thanking God, perhaps, for those diligent and dedicated servants who stay awake on our behalf?

Many people suffer occasional periods of insomnia. But instead of letting that time become festered with anxiety, how wonderful it would be if you would redeem those times by spending them with God. Remember that late one night Jesus asked his disciples, "Could you not keep awake one hour? Keep awake and pray" (Mark 14:37–38). You can do that too.

DAY 156
Read Psalm 135

Here is a robust and celebratory psalm that engages both the intellect and the emotions in its jubilation. Sometimes our praise to God stems from our understanding of what God does, and at other times our celebration of God arises simply from what God is. Some people think their way to God; others follow their hearts to the same goal. There are those who can make an orderly list of the gracious ways in which God has dealt with us. But there are others who cannot reduce God's favor to the nickels and dimes that fit into the cash register drawer of our understanding, but simply crawl up into God's lap and exult in the divine presence.

Although God is really beyond comparison, the psalmist contrasts the essential impotence of idols with the faculties of God through which we may know God and God may know us. "The idols," the psalm points out, "have mouths, but they do not speak; they have eyes, but they do not see; they have ears; but they do not hear" (vv. 15–17). The implication is that our God speaks to us, sees us, and hears us. And it is precisely because of these faculties that God has won our hearts.

To make a once-and-for-all-time demonstration of these divine capabilities, God came to live among us in the person of Jesus Christ. In Christ God speaks to us; in Christ God sees us; and in Christ God hears what we say.

Jesus gave us our marching orders as Christians when he said to the disciples (and to us) in the upper room, "As the Father has sent me, so I send you" (John 20:21). Jesus was God's way of speaking to us, watching us in concern, and hearing the cries of human need in the first century. We are God's way of speaking to the world and watching the human family in compassion and hearing the cries of pain and need in today's world. And the world is judging your God by what they see in you.

You, too, like our Christ, are sent into the world to be God made flesh, truth made audible, love made practical. If God is to be known in your world, as God was known in first-century Jerusalem, it will have to be through your heart caring, your lips speaking, your feet going, your hands helping. God's reputation is in your hands.

DAY 157
Read Psalm 136

The Talmud referred to this psalm as "the Great Hallel," or the Grand Hallelujah, because of its supreme expression of praise to God. It was obviously intended for use in corporate worship, with the leader reading the first line of each verse and the congregation responding with the refrain, "For his steadfast love endures forever." Twenty-six times this line is repeated, until it becomes a kind of mantra, its essential truth taking on a kind of rhythmic cadence that is as much felt as heard.

In congregations of the "free church" tradition, liturgical materials that make use of repetitions are avoided in favor of more straightforward and logical expressions. And there is justification for that. But people who have grown up repeating religious truths in rote form (such as "Holy Mary, Mother of God, pray for us sinners, now and at the hour of our death. Amen.") have unconsciously stored up in their memory bank a sacred realization that comes back to them to inform their consciousness in times of special need. Perhaps there would be some justification for every Christian to compose (or adopt) a short statement of religious truth that can be repeated frequently until it becomes a part of one's spiritual armory. Ideally it should be short, easily remembered, and expressive of a supreme religious truth. It would be difficult to find a better phrase than the one in this psalm that surely served the "mantra" purpose for the ancient Hebrews: "God's steadfast love endures forever."

What can you say when your guilt makes you wonder if you have wandered beyond God's care? "God's steadfast love endures forever." What assurance is there that can give you confidence as you face an uncertain future? "God's steadfast love endures forever." What words can provide the joy that fills the vacancy left by the defection of earthly companions? "God's steadfast love endures forever." What words can relieve the gloom that surrounds the gaping door of death that faces every person? "God's steadfast love endures forever."

Surely every one of us needs some fragment of divine truth that we may hold onto in times of stress or pain or doubt. And surely no truth is of greater importance to us than this, that "God's steadfast love endures forever."

DAY 158
Read Psalm 137

Psalm 137 presents a painful paradox. It begins with one of the most graceful expressions in the whole Bible, and ends with what is surely the most hateful curse to be found in Holy Writ. Who can match the grandeur of the language in which it is written, "By the waters of Babylon, there we sat down and wept, when we remembered Zion" (v. 1, RSV). But nothing can quite prepare us for the shock of hearing the psalmist conclude with the bitter malediction, "Happy shall they be who take your little ones and dash them against the rock!" (v. 9).

And the paradox is that both the sublime and the despicable arose from the same human experience. Many of the Hebrew people (including the psalmist) had been defeated and carried away into involuntary servitude in Babylon. Understandably, they felt the pangs of homesickness for their native Jerusalem. It was more than their home: Jerusalem was also their hope. They had trusted in God to protect them against the onslaught of the pagan invaders. But their defenses had failed them; their city fell, and they were pressed into slavery. One can easily understand their despair and sympathize with their resentment against their masters who ridiculed their faith and demanded them to sing some of their religious songs to entertain their captors. They hung their harps on the willow trees and declared that they would never be able to sing again.

But then homesickness turned to bitterness and hatred, and the beauty of their lament turned sour, and they convicted themselves by their own resentment.

When we are faced with adversity of any kind, we have two alternatives: We can let the experience make us bitter or better. We can grow through disappointment or be dwarfed by it. When Joseph—by then a powerful political leader in Egypt—was reunited with his brothers, he made a striking observation. Instead of spewing venomous resentments that he had been storing up against his brothers for many years, Joseph said to them, "Even though you intended to do harm to me, God intended it for good" (Genesis 50:20). The same human experiences that draw praises from some will draw curses from others. The choice is ours.

Toward the end of this psalm the writer concludes, "The LORD will fulfill the Lord's purpose for me" (v. 8). This assurance carries with it the acknowledgement of three important truths. First, the Lord has a purpose. Despite occasional appearances to the contrary, there is a divine purpose at work in our universe. We are not helpless puppets whose strings are pulled by the winds of blind chance. Although the revelation of God's purpose is too grand a disclosure to be discerned on the small stage of momentary events, the broad scope of history clearly shows the hand of God.

Jesus once told his disciples, "My Father is still working" (John 5:17). Unlike the deists who believe that God completed the divine work before giving human beings complete control over the universe, we believe that God still cares about creation and still intervenes in human affairs to bring the universe into compliance with a heavenly purpose. God has a plan!

The second realization stemming from this assurance of the psalmist is that God's plan will be accomplished. Those who fear that the evil in the world will eventually cause the great conflagration that will end human existence have forgotten one thing: God will not be defeated by evil. If and when the life of the earth ceases, it will not be because God was finally defeated, but because God's purpose was ultimately fulfilled. God's plan will be accomplished, whether with our help or over our objection.

Finally, the declaration of the psalmist indicates that God's plan involves us. "The LORD will fulfill the Lord's purpose *for me*." Somewhere in the vast, all-encompassing plan of God for the universe, there is a part that each of us must play.

A children's story says, "for want of a nail, a shoe was lost," and that that tiny fault grew exponentially, with the eventual result of the loss of a kingdom.

Perhaps that thing that you know you should do, that you know you could do, but that you think is not important enough to do may be the linchpin on which God's plan for your world is delayed or defeated.

"Thy will be done," we pray repeatedly, as though God is waiting for something to happen to make a glorious destiny a reality in our lives. But what if God's will is frustrated by our "won't"?

DAY 160
Read Psalm 139

Do you remember when, as a child, you were frightened by new experiences? Perhaps you stood nervously before a dark cave with a group of playmates. There was an undeniable lure about that shadowy interior. Curiosity drew you toward its mystery, but caution held you back from exploring it. You threw rocks into it and listened to their echoes as they skittered against the dark walls. But none of the rocks came back to tell you what it was really like inside the cave. You had to explore it for yourself. But each child held back, hoping that a more adventuresome playmate would take the first step into the darkness. "You go first. You go first, and I'll follow."

Magnificent Psalm 139 assures us that God has gone before us into every experience of life. If only we could learn to trust God. But there we go, so often running ahead of God, down the road, and calling God to follow us. And the farther ahead of God we go, the more we worry, and the more we have to worry about. No wonder we so often beat our heads against an unyielding wall or pound our fists on doors that will not open, blaming God for failing to follow us where we have chosen to go. But if we follow where God leads, we will never be where God has not gone first, rolling away stones, opening doors, making the unbearable bearable and the impossible possible.

During the Second World War, millions of American youth were dispatched to the farthest corners of the earth, into unfamiliar and often hostile territory, to serve their country. Despite their courage, one can easily imagine the fear and homesickness that often gripped them as they ventured into places and experiences that were new to them. But there was a quaint tradition that gave them some comfort. No one knows exactly how the custom began, but many people experienced it. Everywhere they went, they would find a clumsy drawing with a legend beside it, "Kilroy Was Here!" It was good for a laugh, but even more importantly, it said to them that someone had gone that way before them.

So God has gone this way ahead of us. There is no place we can be that God has not gone first. If we ascend into heaven, God is there! If we make our bed in the grave, God is there! If we take the wings of the morning and dwell in the uttermost parts of the sea, even there God's hand leads us, and God's right hand holds us. The secret to a happy life is to pray, and keep praying every day of your life, "You go first, Lord, and I'll follow."

DAY 161
Read Psalm 140

In the days before television, radio, and moving pictures, people found entertainment in recitations or dramatic readings learned in elocution lessons. Many a social gathering was enlivened by an impassioned delivery of perennial favorites such as "Curfew Shall Not Ring Tonight" or "The Preacher and the Bear." In the latter recitation, the reader assumes the identity of the preacher, out for a hike in the woods, who is confronted by an angry bear. The preacher runs, and the bear pursues. The preacher climbs a tree, only to see the bear following him, limb by limb. In desperation the preacher prays, "Lord, if you can't help me, at least don't help that bear!"

Such is the sentiment of the psalmist in this cry for deliverance. "Do not grant, O Lord, the desires of the wicked" (v. 8). At least don't help them! We are not specifically informed as to the nature of the difficulty confronting the psalmist, but it is clear that he felt gravely threatened by those who wished to do him harm. Although this is not one of the better-known psalms, Paul quoted it in his epistle to the Romans (Romans 3:13). The fact is that in this world the righteous are often threatened by evil and sometimes even defeated by it.

But God comes to the rescue! God provides a way of escape from evil. That is the assurance that is echoed in 1 Corinthians 10:13: "God is faithful, and God will not let you be tested beyond your strength, but with the testing God will also provide the way out so that you may be able to endure it."

The word *deliver* carries with it the sense of being pulled out of a threatening situation. When one is delivered from evil, he or she is not only released from some evil, but also rescued for some good purpose. "Deliver us from evil," we often say in the Lord's Prayer: Out of the darkness and into the light, out of fear and into confidence, out of anxiety and into peace, out of defeat and into victory.

Such is the promise of the God who claims us as children of the Divine. "I have made you and I will bear you; I will carry you and I will save you" (paraphrasing Isaiah 46:4). For such a long way God has been your Lord, your protector, your strong deliverer. What makes you think God will drop you now?

A brief newspaper article from the wires of the Associated Press reported the minor tragedy of an elderly woman who had fallen in her backyard and broken her hip. At first reading the event seemed unremarkable, until the aggravating cause of the fall was reported. She had tripped on the electrified wire she had strung around her prize tomato plants to keep the neighborhood children from raiding her garden. Here was a classic demonstration of the common human experience of being hoisted on one's own petard. (The familiar saying refers to an explosive device used in medieval warfare. It was packed with dangerous explosives but had such a short fuse that the unfortunate one who undertook the lighting of it was often blown up in the process.)

Both the petard and the elderly woman using dangerous means of protecting her tomatoes are examples of people falling into their own traps. And the human experience is full of such examples, because it is an undisputable fact of nature that one cannot perpetrate harm against another without sharing in the product. You can't throw mud at someone without getting your hands dirty!

That is the conclusion of Psalm 141, which ends with the words, "Let the wicked fall into their own nets, while I alone escape" (v. 10). It is a self-fulfilling prayer, for by our actions toward others, we create the world we live in. Jesus raised this dictum to the height of sacred dogma when he said, in what has come to be known as the golden rule, "In everything do to others as you would have them do to you; for this is the law and the prophets" (Matthew 7:12). Those who build traps to ensnare others will learn, by their own sad experiences, what it feels like to fall into a trap. But those who face the world with kindness will find the world responding in kind.

It is regrettable that the psalmist expressed this truth in the nature of a threat to the evildoers who intimidated him. Even acts of apparent kindness can become weapons of bitterness and resentment. And although it is true that trap-makers will eventually become trapped in their own devices, such a fate is not ours to bestow. "Vengeance is mine," says the Lord. "I will repay" (Romans 12:19).

DAY 163
Read Psalm 142

"Nobody knows the troubles I've seen," runs the familiar spiritual, and it evokes a feeling with which all of us are familiar. In times of distress, the walls that confine us narrow, and we feel trapped. On such occasions, it is often true that we feel absolutely alone and that nobody knows us, nobody cares about us, and nobody will help us.

Several years ago an American submarine experienced an explosion that left a gaping hole in the hull of the ship and destroyed all the lines of communication between those on board and the outside world. Skilled crew members began the task of sealing the hole in the ship's side, but in those tense moments until the ship was restored to a safe condition, those on board feared that they were facing their peril alone. They could not receive any messages, but they kept broadcasting their pleas for help, not knowing whether the messages were being received. Again and again they radioed the plaintive call, "Is anybody there? Does anybody know we're here? Does anybody care?"

Fortunately, a nearby ship received those messages, and help was even then on the way to rescue the threatened sailors. But the words of their melancholy fears kept reproaching the silence: "Is anybody there? Does anybody know we're here? Does anybody care?"

Such an experience provides a painful reminder of those times when our adversities isolate us and make us fear that we are facing our problems without help and without even a caring notice from others. But at such times we need to be reminded that help is on the way.

In Jesus' story of the good Samaritan we see the pitiable figure of a man, wounded and robbed, left for dead beside the road. From the distance of the years between Jesus' story and our hearing of it, we know that help would come—not perhaps the help he might have expected (the priest and Levite, whose religious beliefs might have compelled them to help), but help came nonetheless.

One of our favorite old hymns says:

Do your friends despise, forsake you?
Take it to the Lord in prayer.
In his arms he'll take and shield you;
you will find a solace there.

You are not alone!

DAY 164
Read Psalm 143

The early church defined seven psalms as "penitential" and found them useful in reminding people of their sinful nature and their need of divine grace. This is one of those psalms.

It begins with the acknowledgement that it is because of God's own faithfulness and righteousness that we may expect from God more than we deserve. God does not deal with us according to our worth, but according to God's nature and our need. The psalmist does not plead for justice, for none of us would be found guiltless in a court of divine justice. This understanding was the foundation stone of Paul's theology. He wrote, "All have sinned and fall short of the glory of God; they are now justified by his grace as a gift, through the redemption that is in Christ Jesus" (Romans 3:23–24). That was precisely what David wanted, needed, prayed for, but what he could only hope would somehow be available to him.

But what was only a deeply felt hope for David in Old Testament times became a radiant fact in New Testament times because of the redemptive sacrifice of Jesus Christ. Like David, we long for, pray for, base our hopes on the possibility that God will deal with us with amazing grace. But like Paul we rejoice that such a hope has been confirmed!

There is another hint of the glorious understanding of God that Jesus would reveal, in the tenth verse of this psalm, which pleads with God, "Let your good spirit lead me on a level path." Several centuries would pass before David's prayer would be answered by a Christ, meeting with his disciples in the upper room on the night before his death and giving them the promise of "a good spirit" from God that would lead us into all righteousness. He said, "When the Spirit of truth comes, he will guide you into all the truth" (John 16:13).

But that "good spirit" invites, guides, encourages, and affirms. The good spirit pulls us but never pushes us. And the "level path" along which the spirit guides us is not a free-for-all ride down a slippery slope or a treacherous climb up a perilous mountain. It is a level path, which requires our cooperation with the gentle tug of God's presence.

The Old Testament acknowledges the two major expressions of God's activity: deliverance and blessing. God rescues us, and God provides for us. In this psalm there is a reiteration of these two shapes of God's divine conduct.

The latter half of the psalm (vv. 12–15) depicts the happiness of the human family within the context of the *shalom* that was God's intention for the world. The words are reminiscent of Shakespeare's words in *Henry V,* "We few; we happy few; we band of brothers." In the words of the psalm, all the people of the earth are seen as a family, with brothers and sisters, sons and daughters, old and young. And the bountiful crops and the healthy livestock help to create a society of peace in which there is no cry of distress in the streets. "Happy are the people to whom such blessings fall" (v. 15). And such blessings result from the realization of the people that they belong to God.

There is almost a hint of insular coziness here. "Let the heathens suffer their want and pain. As for us, we are the Lord's people, and therefore we are blessed." At first it sounds like the self-centered prayer of one man: "God bless just only me, that's as far as I can see."

But in fact it was God's intention that all people should regard themselves as a family, sharing blessings and burdens, in a society in which all needs are met and all gifts are utilized. And whether we regard all people as children of God, it is clearly God's intention that all should claim such a distinction.

It was with sadness that God put the question to Cain, "Where is your brother?" Cain's flippant reply, "Am I my brother's keeper?" was irrelevant (Genesis 4:9). What was more important was that he was his brother's *brother.*

And as long as we live in a world in which many suffer want and pain, there can be no *shalom,* no "happy family" embracing all humankind. Injustice for the many convicts the greed of the few. And we will not be a "band of brothers" until "we few, we happy few" extend the walls of our house to include all whom God regards as children of the Holy.

"God is great. God is good. Let us thank him for our food." So runs the prayer before a meal, learned in our childhood. It might well be thought of as a summary of this beautiful psalm, which was used by Hebrew families for many centuries as an expression of gratitude for the abundance of food that the Lord provides.

God is great. That fact had been clearly demonstrated in the history of Israel and its individual citizens. The rescue of Israel from the iron grip of the Egyptian pharaoh, the miraculous escape through the Red Sea on dry land, the daily sustenance of the pilgrims through their forty years of wandering through the wilderness of Sinai, and the conquest and occupation of the promised land were often cited as evidences of God's greatness.

But, as the saying goes, that was then; this is now. What catalog of blessings in your own life might be listed as proofs of the greatness of God? To perpetrate a twist on a frequently-asked question, "If God were accused in a court of law of being a great God, would there be enough evidence to make a conviction?" What has God been up to in your own life, achieving victories and accomplishing miracles that would have been impossible in your own strength and abilities?

Yet God is not only "great" but also "good." "The LORD is gracious and merciful, slow to anger and abounding in steadfast love" (v. 8). And in a deceptively simple statement we are reminded, "The LORD is good to all, and his compassion is over all that he has made" (v. 9). We are dealing with a God who is not only good to us, but to every person.

It can be comforting for us to realize that God loves us. But sometimes it comes as a great shock to us to learn that God loves other people, too—quite as much as God loves us. Sometimes we wish it were not so. Sometimes we wish God would hate our enemies as much as we do. But if there were, in God's heart, the capability of despising anyone, we might ourselves be victimized by the capriciousness in which God might decide to drop someone from the divine burden of compassion. But because God is good to everyone, we know that includes us. "Be perfect," Jesus said, "as your heavenly Father is perfect" (Matthew 5:48). By that Jesus did not call us to moral perfection, but to a complete, leave-no-one-out concern in which no human being is left behind. It is in that astonishing assurance that we can find the confidence to know that the great God will be good—in every way—even to the least of us.

DAY 167
Read Psalm 146

The last five psalms are all "praise psalms." Each begins and ends with the phrase "Praise the LORD," or "Hallelujah!" in the original Hebrew. Taken together, they form a doxology that provides a brilliant climax to a collection of conversations with God, in which a variety of emotions and concerns have been expressed. And God does not turn a deaf ear to any cry for help. But what a blessing is to be derived from recognizing and celebrating the praiseworthiness of our God!

The gospel of Luke ends with a most provocative statement. Jesus had ascended into heaven, leaving his followers with the most demanding commission ever given to a group of frail and faulty human beings: to go into all the world and make disciples of all the nations. What a responsibility! What a burden! Surely they must get busy! There was no time to lose!

So how did thy go about fulfilling that magnificent obsession? The scripture says of those burdened disciples, "they were continually in the temple blessing God" (Luke 24:53). A waste of time? Ah, no! They knew that the challenge they faced deserved and required them to be at their very best. They recognized that they were being asked to accomplish a mission impossible. So to sharpen their abilities and deepen their dedication and invigorate their energies, they needed to establish clearly the resource by which they would go into all the world. That resource was their close and never-failing relationship with the living God. And it was in that "continually in the temple blessing God" that they received the spiritual energy and incentive to accomplish their work.

There is a lovely Spanish word that falls from the lips with grace and beauty: *accumuladora*. What a lilt there is in the mere articulation of that musical word! But its meaning is quite mundane: It means "battery." What it says is that energy has been accumulated that can be tapped whenever and wherever energy is needed.

So blessing God, recognizing the goodness and greatness of God, thanking and praising God become the *accumuladora* of the Christian. Before we can "do," we must "become." And to become what we need to become, to be able to do what we should do as Christians, we need the experience of praising God.

DAY 168
Read Psalm 147

In the middle of this psalm, in which God's hand is seen at work in the natural world, there is a curious mention of young ravens, crying for food. There is an interesting bit of fact and tradition expressed in that brief mention. Ravens were regarded with disgust among the ancient Hebrews, who considered them "unclean" because they feasted on carrion. Ravens were not accepted as temple sacrifices and were never kept as pets.

But note this: It was ravens who fed Elijah bread and flesh, every morning and every evening, when the prophet sought refuge in the desert at the brook of Cherith.

And this: The Hebrew word for raven had exactly the same arrangement of consonants as the word for Arab. And because no vowels were used in recording the Old Testament text, we are left to wonder whether the unexpected kindness to Elijah in the desert was provided by ravens or by Arabs, both of which were despised and distrusted by the Israelites.

Tradition offers the explanation that ravens were despised because they abandoned the nest of hatchlings soon after their birth, leaving their offspring (which are white, and not black, at birth) to fend for themselves. Untrue though this tradition may be, it is nevertheless perpetuated in the German word for an unfit mother who abandons her children: *Rabenmutter,* "raven mother."

But the psalm specifically singles out the nest of young ravens as recipients of the mercy and provision of God. And Jesus said, "Consider the ravens: they neither sow nor reap, they have neither storehouse nor barn, and yet God feeds them" (Luke 12:24). And here in this psalm is the tender picture, "[God] gives to the animals their food, and to the young ravens when they cry" (v. 9).

Have you ever been falsely slandered, or abandoned by those who should care about you, or hungry for food or for nourishment for the spirit that nobody seems willing to provide. Take heart! The Lord hears your cry and will give you what you need.

In connection with this psalm, in his commentary on the Psalms, James Limburg quoted a poem by Gerhard Frost:

> We sat together,
> This tall man and a tiny child,
> Before the fireplace.
> Enthralled with this, her first,
> And looking up at me,
> She said, "It's clapping."
> I would have said, "It's crackling,"
> And so would you—
> Victims of the dulling years—
> But who is right?
> Who has really heard?
> Can fire praise by crackling?
> No, she's the one
> Who has found the word.
> Indeed, it's clapping,
> "Praise the Lord."
> (from *Blessed Is the Ordinary*)

We are grateful to both the poet and the scholar who brought this tender picture to our minds. The child was right: The fire was clapping, applauding its progenitor for the gift of its fire-ness. The fire praises its creator by being fire. The sea monsters, and hail and snow, and people of all ages and stages of life praise God by being what God made them to be. We need not be a star or a planet or a majestic mountain or sparkling brook to reflect God's glory. "The glory of God is in man fully alive," wrote the theologian. And every created thing joins a chorus of praise that sings an anthem of thanksgiving to the source of all life.

Praise the Lord!

DAY 170
Read Psalm 149

This next-to-last psalm is filled with images of joy and happiness. "Let Israel be glad," it says (v. 2), and the people of God are invited to express their exultation in singing, dancing, and playing musical instruments. Surely the greatness and goodness of our God should be sufficient cause for rejoicing.

But echoing this joy of the people, we read of God that "the LORD takes pleasure in the Lord's people" (v. 4). Did that thought ever occur to you, that God enjoys us?

So often, prompted, perhaps, by our chronic sense of guilt and worthlessness, we think of God as bearing an expression like that of the Man of La Mancha–the knight of the doleful countenance. Surely God is disgusted with our frailties, disappointed by our failures, and almost at the point of abandoning us as hopeless. But there is another view of God that this psalm expresses. Frail and faulty as we are, God takes pleasure in us.

In the traditional Christmas story as reported by Luke, many people were disappointed by the *New Revised Standard Version* (NRSV) of the New Testament, which abandons the old wording of the angel's message ("on earth peace, good will toward men" [Luke 2:14, KJV]). Although less lyrical, perhaps, the NRSV rendition is more accurate: "on earth peace among those whom God favors." What a relief! Instead of just barely holding onto us because of our failures, God hugs us to God's heart in joyful abandon. God is pleased with us! Or, as the psalm puts it, "The LORD takes pleasure in his people."

Listen, child of God: You may be riddled with doubts, stained with the guilt of a thousand misdeeds, unable to bring enough conviction to God that promises a brighter future than your past. Nevertheless, God–who knows you even better than you know yourself–finds pleasure in you. You matter to God. If God had a refrigerator, your picture would be on its door.

David, who was possibly the writer of this psalm, had surely provided God with enough reasons to cast him into a lake of fire forever. Nevertheless, he knew the mind and heart of God enough to pray, "Guard me as the apple of the eye" (Psalm 17:8).

A child came home from Sunday school troubled by the memory verse for the day, "Thou God seest me" (Genesis 16:13, KJV). It sounded so stern, like a policeman watching a suspect for any sign of lawbreaking. Her parents solved the problem by re-translating the verse to make it say, "God loves you so much God can't keep his eyes off you."

And that's how God feels about you. "The LORD takes pleasure in his people."

The book of Psalms ends with a wild, joyous outburst of grateful praise that shakes the rafters of our reverence and reverberates throughout our systematic theology and sends shock waves through our narrow view of what constitutes the community of God's people. Listen as it builds in force and enthusiasm:

> Praise the LORD!
> Praise God in his sanctuary! (v. 1)

(So far, so good, if we could just agree on which of the great temples we regularly meet in is really God's sanctuary!)

> Praise him for his mighty deeds;
> Praise him according to his surpassing greatness! (v. 2)

(We certainly can't argue with that, for even the most grumbling and picky of us can surely discern that surpassing greatness of the outpouring of God's blessings to us. If only God were a bit more selective in distributing God's gifts. Making the sun to shine on the evil, as well as the good, and the rain to fall on the just, as well as the unjust, occasionally seems a bit sloppy to us, as though God weren't too good in aiming.)

Then the psalmist calls together the great symphony orchestra to play this overture of thankful praise:

> Praise him with trumpet sound; praise him with lute and harp!
> Praise him with tambourine and dance; praise him with strings and pipe!
> Praise him with clanging cymbals; praise him with loud clashing cymbals! (vv. 3–5)

Then, having achieved that fever pitch of joyous abandon in this song of praise, the psalmist pulls out all the stops and stretches the capacity of our listening hearts to hear the climactic crescendo:

> Let everything that breathes praise the LORD! (v. 6)

Everything that breathes? Yes, everything that breathes is the creation of our God, and for our God to be properly praised, adequately adored, and truly thanked requires a greater chorus of voices than usually convenes to sing God's praise. And every worship service is only a rehearsal for the grand event, what Pierre Teilhard de Chardin called "the Omega Point," at which time all creatures will know that they are God's and will join in this grand anthem of praise to our God.

Also by C. William Nichols

We hope you enjoy the excerpts on the following pages from these other inspirational books:

Day by Day

through the NEW TESTAMENT

THE GOSPELS

C. William Nichols

0-8272-0628-3

Day by Day

through the NEW TESTAMENT

ACTS to
REVELATION

C. William Nichols

0-8272-0629-1

DAY 1
Read Matthew 1:1–17

What a dirty trick to play on someone who has decided to undertake a reading of the New Testament! With all the inspiration and guidance in their repertoire of teachings, why must the biblical writers confront us, on the very first page, with a dry-as-dust listing of the ancestors of Jesus? Who cares who Jehoshaphat was (except perhaps to wonder how he came to be remembered as "Jumpin'")? What does Zerubbabel have to contribute to the matchless story of the one who is remembered as earth's best good news? The gospel writers can thrill us with the most graceful and forceful writing the world has ever read—except "when they begin the Begats!"

A moment's thought, however, gives us a clue to the genius of Matthew in beginning his gospel in this fashion. Each person whose name is listed in this pedigree may seem unimportant to us, from our later perspective of all these generations. But each one named there was created in the image of God, and, for the length of one life span, was the link joining the past to the future. In his or her own time, each one fulfilled the function of carrying forward the gifts and graces (as well as the flaws and faults) of the previous generations, adding to them, and passing on the whole bundle of potential that (with God's help) eventually resulted in the one we know as the Lord of all life.

Note that not all the people whom Jesus could claim as ancestors were pure and pious. There were some real swingers hanging from the branches of Jesus' family tree. Jacob was there—scheming, conniving Jacob, who cheated his old blind father and swindled his brother Esau out of what properly belonged to him. Ahaz was among Jesus' progenitors—remembered mostly as the king who gave to foreign potentates the rich ornaments of the temple, and even burned his own son to death. In a classic understatement, the Bible says of him, "and he did not do what was right in the eyes of the Lord." Among the women cited in this genealogy, two were of foreign blood, and one was a prostitute.

Yet from that lineage was born God's greatest gift! Matthew's reminder, through this listing of Jesus' ancestors, is that God can take any material that is available and make something magnificent of it. As God once took the clay of the ground and breathed into it the breath of life, producing a human being in the image of the Creator, so God can take your life—as flawed and impoverished of virtue as you may feel—and make you a miracle of grace.

A small boy came home from Sunday school in tears. His parents questioned him and learned that the cause of the tears was the part he had been assigned in the Christmas pageant. Between sobs he informed them that he had been given the part of Joseph. His parents tried to console him by explaining, "But Joseph was one of the major characters in the Christmas story. He was the father of Jesus." "I know," the boy wailed, "but I wanted to have a speaking part."

And he was right. Nowhere in the gospels is Joseph quoted. In the Christmas story, Mary speaks eloquent volumes, as does her cousin Elizabeth. Zechariah, once he found his tongue after the shock of his own incipient miracle had initially struck him dumb, waxed lyrical in his celebration. The Judean shepherds found something to say in this story, as did the wise men from the East. Even perfidious old King Herod had a speaking part, but not Joseph.

Who can underestimate the importance of Joseph's contribution, though? Surely God sought a father for the Messiah child, as carefully as God had selected the one who was to mother him. Even before the angel's announcement to Joseph, he is shown to be a person of integrity, inclined by a lifetime of habit to "do the right thing." In this case, doing the right thing meant to divorce a fiancée who was found to be pregnant, though not by him. That was the right thing–legally. But shining through what would have been a drab fulfillment of human law was a touch of grace. Joseph resolved to give her the privacy of his discretion to spare her the pain of public scrutiny. Often there is something more right than "right," and that is mercy.

Then in a dream Joseph received the news that Mary was pregnant with the child of the Holy Spirit. And he believed that word! Incredible as it may have seemed, and as much as it must have cost Joseph, he was willing to trust the tiny light of inspiration that came to him, and live by it.

Jesus was later to say, "Blessed are those who have not seen and yet have come to believe" (John 20:29). And in those words he gave a benediction to his human father, whose blind trust provided the secure family life into which God could safely send the Redeemer.

DAY 3
Read Matthew 2:1–12

Matthew was eager to prove, through his gospel treatise, that Jesus was the fulfillment of the centuries-old Jewish dream of a Messiah, and that, further, this Messiah would sit on the historic throne of David and be the royal king of the Jews. What better way to begin his story, then, than to cite all those Old Testament prophecies that seemed perfectly fulfilled in the events of Jesus' nativity! How impoverished we would be without Matthew's reporting of events that are nowhere else mentioned, such as the appearance of a star, hinted at by Balaam's prophecy: "A star shall come out of Jacob" (Numbers 24:17). What better way to prove that Jesus was a king from birth than to record the visit of the wise men, who presented the Bethlehem baby with gifts befitting a king?

Little is known of those mysterious magi. We don't know how many there were. Tradition has said there were three–probably concluded from the number of gifts that were presented. They were probably not kings, but rather court astrologers or magicians, from somewhere to the east of Bethlehem. (They said that it was "in the East" that they had first seen the star.)

Those mysterious magi earned the esteem in which they are held in Christian tradition because they recognized divine guidance when they saw it, and followed it, even when they couldn't see it. Contrary to our usual understanding of their journey, they did not have the benefit of the star's constant guidance. They caught a glimpse of it "at its rising," or at the beginning of their following it. But shortly after they had begun their journey, apparently, the star disappeared, and they did not see it again until after they left Jerusalem. No wonder they were "overwhelmed with joy," when they could see it again, for it was their first sighting of the star since their journey had begun. There must have been many long desert stretches of nothing along the way–no inspiration, no guidance, no confirming evidence that they were going in the right direction. But they continued in the direction remembered from their first sighting, until, at last, they found the Christ child.

How easy life would be if only some brilliant star constantly showed us the right path! Unfortunately, most of our discipleship takes place not when we can see the star, but when we can't, when despite our discouragement or spiritual weariness we must continue to follow the remembered stars of those times of clear days when we could see forever.

DAY 4
Read Matthew 2:13–23

The last chapter of the Christmas story according to Matthew reminds us that the Christ came into a world in which promises are broken, babies die, powerful people do unjust things, and families sometimes lose their homes to become political refugees. It is a cruel world into which the Savior was born, a world of sin. And that is, of course, precisely why the world needed a savior in the first place.

Despite the enormous gulf that exists between the righteousness of God and the sinfulness of the world, the Christmas event describes the manner in which God bridged that gulf. Christ was that "bridge over troubled water," the one in whom heaven and earth met. Paul marveled at this unique ministry that only Christ could render, and said, "In Christ God was reconciling the world to himself" (2 Corinthians 5:19).

The last chapter of the Christmas story also proves to us that the joy of the Christ event does not require the quiet serenity of a monastery to be experienced. Christ comes to us not only when our souls are enjoying reverent repose but also when we face the ragged edges of human pain and grief. Christ is at home in our sorrow and danger, having faced those experiences in his own life, beginning even in his infancy, when his parents became displaced persons, to escape Herod's cruelty.

The good news of Christmas is that Christ is not conquered even by such extremities of human experience. Often only when we experience such dark times is the light of Christ's presence most clearly comprehended. As the stars cannot be seen until the darkness comes, much of Christ's helpful presence we cannot know when life is easy and untroubled.

Tommy was afraid of the dark, despite his mother's repeated assurance that there was nothing in the dark that would harm him. One day she asked Tommy to go down into the basement and bring her a can of tomato soup from the pantry shelves in the dark room below. Tommy opened the door and peered uncertainly into the unlit basement. "Don't be afraid," his mother told him. "Jesus will be down there with you." "Jesus," Tommy said, "if you're down there, please hand me a can of tomato soup."

It is comforting to us to know that whatever we face, Jesus will face it with us, and that he has already overcome that same extremity in his own human life.

DAY 5
Read Matthew 3

No one had ambivalent feelings toward John, the son of Zechariah and Elizabeth. They either flocked to his wilderness sanctuary, like moths to a flame, to hear his stern, no-holds-barred lectures, or they hated him enough to imprison him, and subsequently behead him.

John was a phenomenon—a paradox misunderstood then and now. He was part clown and part prophet; part aesthete and part pragmatist. A sartorial buffoon and gustatorial disgrace, he was what Paul might have called a "fool for the sake of Christ" (1 Corinthians 4:10). And one suspects that John would gladly have accepted the sobriquet and worn it as a crown, provided the words "for the sake of Christ" remained intact.

He came roaring out of the desert with the single-minded purpose of preparing the world to receive its Christ. He called those of easy virtue to repent, and he did not dilute his message of judgment even when it pointed accusingly at those whose power could loose its fury against him—and ultimately did.

He modestly rejected the attempts of the crowds to elect him Messiah, and he made his own function clear: He was the introducer of Christ, the scene-setter, the warm-up act, the one who would know the high privilege of baptizing the Messiah and the depths of despair of counting the hours, in Herod's dungeon, until his head would be served up on a platter to pamper a dancing girl's whim. He was the one whose long-anticipated words, "Behold the Lamb of God, who takes away the sin of the world," continue to ring in the ears of a world that still needs to behold and receive and know the one John gave his life to herald.

Every one of us has what might be called a representative capacity—the ability to manifest or depict, in our life, some quality or entity or person outside ourselves. Each of us is like a flagpole. Some flagpoles are tall and straight and strong; others are crooked and weak; some are ornate, others are plain. But the glory of a flagpole lies not in what it is but in the colors that it flies.

So, like a plain wire grown incandescent, it is possible for us to glow with whatever it is that possesses us. As Paul was able to say, "It is no longer I who live, but it is Christ who lives in me" (Galatians 2:20). So John was alive with Christ. And so are you, when Christ's Spirit inhabits your life.

DAY 1
Read Acts 1

In their final meeting with Jesus, the disciples showed how much they needed the experience of a time of prayer and preparation before they were ready to represent the Christ to a world that did not know him. With a new ethic of love and a new promise of wholeness to proclaim to a needy world, their only question was a political one: "Lord, is this time when you will restore the kingdom to Israel?" It was almost in exasperation that Jesus replied, "It is not for you to know the times or periods that the Father has set by his own authority."

It was as if Jesus were saying to his followers, "That is not your business. That is God's business. God will handle it." But then Jesus told them what their business was: "But you will receive power when the Holy Spirit has come upon you; and you will be my witnesses." There was a magnificent obsession that would consume the rest of their lives—to go into all the world and proclaim the gospel of Christ. But before they were ready to begin that historic endeavor, they must first receive from God the power by which they would be capable of doing it.

In our pragmatic and activist age, being a Christian is frequently seen as a matter of doing the right thing and making the most helpful contributions to a world that limps along in its discovery of the divine purpose. And certainly all our best efforts are needed and justified. But Christianity is not so much something that we do, as something that we are, and only then what we do as a result of what we are.

A teacher in a missionary school for boys in India was well known for his patience, even in the most trying circumstances. He was often asked where he got his patience. He always replied, somewhat cryptically, "It grows in my garden." One day a group of his students showed up at his house and demanded to see that famous garden where such amazing patience grew. The teacher led them through his house, out the back door, and into a narrow, cheerless enclosure. When the students expressed disappointment in its lack of beauty and character, the teacher replied, "No, it is not very long, and not very wide. But," he added as he lifted his eyes heavenward, "it is very, very tall."

Don't neglect that garden where your faith grows.

The strange and exciting events of Pentecost had roots that ran back, through misty memory, to an ancient time, a common problem, and a helpful suggestion from an unlikely source. The place was the wilderness of Sinai in the odyssey of the people of Israel from Egypt's bondage to their promised land. Moses, though still a wise and vigorous leader in his eighth decade of life, was finding it difficult to settle all the petty disputes of the contentious people he undertook to lead. Seeing his frustration and weariness, Jethro—Moses' father-in-law—urged Moses to appoint good and wise leaders who would share the burden of responsibility. So Moses, after consulting God in prayer, appointed seventy "elders," who would constitute the board of leadership (later to be known as the Sanhedrin.) Each of the seventy was given a special portion of God's grace to equip him for his leadership role.

But while these seventy fulfilled their divinely appointed role and spoke on God's behalf as prophets, there were two other men of faith—Eldad and Medad—who also spoke on God's behalf and taught the people. Naturally, the regularly appointed elders were offended by the unauthorized actions of these imposters, and appealed to Moses to command them to cease their prophesying. They were not members of the union! They did not carry the proper credentials!

But Moses demonstrated magnanimity and perhaps a glimpse into God's ultimate plan when he answered their complaints, "Would that all the LORD's people were prophets, and that the LORD would put his spirit on them!" (Numbers 11:29). How wonderful it would be if every person were a priest, a prophet endowed by the Holy Spirit! Such was Moses' dream.

Centuries later, the prophet Joel picked up the refrain of Moses' dream, and foretold the day when it would become a reality. "Then afterward," Joel said, "I will pour out my spirit on all flesh; your sons and your daughters shall prophesy, your old men shall dream dreams, and your young men shall see visions" (Joel 2:28).

And at last on the day of Pentecost, the dream of Moses and the vision of Joel became fact! It is the plan and the intention of God that every person should be given the gift of holy endowment and the challenge of divine purpose.

Whatever else may have been accomplished in that historic and eventful day of the church's birth, it also issued you the license that gives you the power and the promise of the Holy God, to act on God's behalf in this world. Claim your inheritance!

DAY 3
Read Acts 3

It was a most dramatic and instructive event: the healing of the lame man at the gate of the temple in Jerusalem. It was the first time a miracle of healing was attributed to followers of Jesus. But note that Peter and John were quick to point out that the credit for the healing did not belong to them, but to the one in whose name the miracle was performed. They said to the curious crowd that gathered around the scene of the healing, "You Israelites, why do you wonder at this, or why do you stare at us, as though by our own power or piety we had made him walk?" "In the name of Jesus Christ of Nazareth," they had said, as the healing took place.

It was an important principle, and one that had to be restated again and again, as the followers of Jesus accomplished works that appeared to be quite beyond the reach of human strength or piety. It was not their power, but Christ's; it was not their righteousness, but the Lord's. They were simply instruments in the transmitting of divine grace to answer human need.

But rather than diminishing their role in this process, Peter and John acknowledged one of the most glorious privileges of our discipleship: that God is willing to condescend to us, to give us access to powers not deserved by our own faith or character. But note this: such powers are given to us only when we are representing God in providing for someone else's needs.

One of the great foundation stones of the Christian movement—and one that was restated in the Protestant Reformation—is the priesthood of every believer. Those tongues of fire—representing the endowment of the Holy Spirit—rested on the heads of all who were present. We do not know how many people were present, or what their experience with Christ had been. But it is clear that such a manifestation was not limited to the apostles. And in that great text from Joel, upon which Peter based his sermon, God had said, "I will pour out my spirit upon all flesh"—all people!

Imagine the honor, the absolute glory, of being a link between divine grace and human need. And that audacious glory is ours when we let ourselves be used as tools in God's hand—"instruments," as St. Francis put it in his memorable prayer, "of thy peace."

And it is that glorious privilege that Pentecost reveals to you.

DAY 4
Read Acts 4

Very early in its history, the church began to experience the persecutions of an establishment that felt threatened by the new spirit demonstrated so magnificently in the lives and actions of the early Christians. The new is always subjected to the paranoia of the old. And the spectacular event of the healing of a lame man at the gate of the temple was the spark that detonated the resentment of the Jewish authorities that had been growing ever since Jesus had first publicly questioned their monopolistic claim on the truth.

The authorities seemed to have all the ammunition on their side. Peter and John—and most of the other Christians—were common people, with little education or theological sophistication. Their experience in religious matters was scarcely three years long. They could not have hoped to win any debates with their adversaries. They had no precedents to offer, no history of ecclesiastical connection. But they had two assets, which assured them of victory against their accusers.

First, they had the evidence of a man who had clearly been healed. When the establishmentarians, in their robes of office, approached Peter and John in the temple, they saw, standing with them, the man who had been healed. And when they saw him standing, on two good and strong legs, in their midst, they had nothing to say in opposition. Results always speak more loudly than any words. The early Christians won their case, time and time again, not by brilliant argument, but by unquestionable results.

The way of Christ works. It did then, and it does now. There is a host of empirical evidence to support that claim, and most of us would have to look no further than our own lives to discover it.

But the disciples had another asset that gave them confidence, and the Jewish authorities recognized it. When they saw the boldness of Peter and John, they recognized that they had been with Jesus. That's the point! They had spent hours in the presence of the Christ, and something in that association had given them qualities of character and a strength of purpose that were beyond the reach of human achievement.

Can your family and friends tell, from your manner, your speech, your actions, that you have spent time with your Lord?

DAY 5
Read Acts 5

As vigorously as science condemns superstition, one must concede that behind some of the cautionary superstitions there may be a grain of truth. Walking under a ladder might, indeed, presage "bad luck," unless you consider the possibility of getting a bucket of paint dropped on your head "good luck." And breaking a mirror does, indeed, result in the misfortune of having to go out and purchase a new one.

So, before we ridicule those who, according to the scriptural record, crowded around Peter in the hope that the shadow of this good man might fall upon them, let us consider what grain of truth might have impelled them to do such a thing. To get within the range of the shadow of Peter meant, obviously, that they had to bring themselves close to him. And being close to Peter would surely result in being influenced by his faith and sharing in the radiance of his transformed personality. There was no magic here, only the natural consequence of companionship with someone of great spiritual stature.

There is no report of any beneficial result of this closeness to Peter, but one must conclude that those upon whom the shadow of Peter fell would derive some blessing from that closeness.

There are two ways to look at this phenomenon. First, we must recognize that there is a magnificent effect stemming from our closeness to people of piety and power. We tend to assume a likeness to those whom we admire enough to seek their presence. When we spend time in the presence of intelligent people, we begin to share in their perceptions. When we are in company with those who are pure in heart, our lives begin to take on their virtues.

But we are also reminded, by the tiny detail in this scripture, of the unconscious influence our presence will have upon those who are close enough to us that our shadow falls on them. Think of those who will be near enough to you today that your shadow falls on them: members of your family, your coworkers, your neighbors, those who may be looking to you for some help. Will your shadow bless them?

Also by C. William Nichols

Day by Day

through the NEW TESTAMENT

THE GOSPELS

C. William Nichols

0-8272-0628-3

Day by Day

through the NEW TESTAMENT

ACTS to
REVELATION

C. William Nichols

0-8272-0629-1